T0147013

THE DEMOCRATIC PARADOX

Radical Thinkers ▼

THE DEMOCRATIC PARADOX

Chantal Mouffe

VERSO

London • New York

First published by Verso 2005
© Chantal Mouffe 2000
Reprinted 2009
All rights reserved

3 5 7 9 10 8 6 4

Verso
UK: 6 Meard Street, London W1F 0EG
US: 20 Jay Street, Suite 1010, Brooklyn, NY 11201
www.versobooks.com

Verso is the imprint of New Left Books

ISBN-13: 978-1-84467-355-1

British Library Cataloguing in Publication Data
A catalogue record for this book is available from the British Library

Library of Congress Cataloging-in-Publication Data
A catalog record for this book is available from the Library of Congress

Typeset by Servis Filmsetting Ltd, Manchester
Printed in the USA

C'est par le malentendu universel que tout le monde s'accorde

Charles Baudelaire

Caminante, no hay camino,
Se hace camino al andar

Antonio Machato

CONTENTS

ACKNOWLEDGMENTS

The articles in this volume were originally published as follows: 'Democracy, Power and "The Political"' in a slightly different version under the title 'Democracy and Pluralism: A Critique of the Rationalist Approach' in *Cardozo Law Review*, 16, 5, March 1995; 'Carl Schmitt and the Paradox of Liberal Democracy' in *The Canadian Journal of Law and Jurisprudence*, X, 1, January 1997; 'For an Agonistic Model of Democracy', in a slightly different version, was written for publication in *Political Theory in Transition*, edited by Noel O'Sullivan (Routledge, 2000); 'A Politics without Adversary?', in a different version under the title 'The Radical Centre: A Politics without Adversary', in *Soundings*, 9, Summer 1998. 'Wittgenstein, Political Theory and Democracy' is the development of a paper presented at a conference at the University of Bielefeld in January 1996.

I wish to thank Daniel Hahn for his editorial assistance.

FOREWORD

The essays collected in this volume have been written in the last five years. Most of them have already been published, some in a different version. One of them, a paper given at a conference, appears here for the first time. The introduction and the conclusion were written especially for the book but incorporate ideas developed in several articles which are not included.

I am conscious that, as far as some of the central themes are concerned, there is a certain amount of reiteration. If I have decided to leave them in their original form, it is because it would have been impossible to eliminate those repetitions without affecting the intelligibility of the argument made in each piece.

The issues discussed in *The Democratic Paradox* constitute the continuation of a reflection initiated jointly with Ernesto Laclau in *Hegemony and Socialist Strategy* and later pursued in *The Return of the Political*. The political events which have taken place since this last book was published, with a growing tendency for social-democratic parties to move towards a consensual politics of the centre, have reinforced my conviction that it is urgent for political theory to provide an alternative framework to the dominant one in democratic political theory. Grasping the fundamental flaws at the core of the 'third way' requires coming to terms with the conflictual nature of politics and the ineradicability of antagonism, which is precisely what the increasingly fashionable 'deliberative democracy' approach is at pains to deny.

It was while reading these texts again for publication that I realized that, albeit in different ways, all of them were highlighting the paradoxical nature of modern liberal democracy. Since the distaste for paradoxes is widespread among the rationalist thinkers with whom I am arguing, I decided that this was the aspect of my current work worth emphasizing. Hence the title of this volume.

INTRODUCTION

THE DEMOCRATIC PARADOX

Albeit in different ways, all the essays collected in this volume deal with what I call 'the paradox' of modern democracy and they try to examine its diverse political and theoretical implications. My reflection begins with an enquiry into the nature of modern democracy, which I think is far from having been properly elucidated. To start with, what is the best way to designate the new type of democracy established in the West in the course of the last two centuries? A variety of terms have been used: modern democracy, representative democracy, parliamentary democracy, pluralist democracy, constitutional democracy, liberal democracy. For some people, the main difference with ancient democracy lies in the fact that in larger and more complex societies direct forms of democratic rule are no longer possible; it is for that reason that modern democracy has to be representative. Others, like Claude Lefort, insist on the symbolic transformation which made possible the advent of modern democracy: 'the dissolution of the markers of certainty'.[1] In his view, modern democratic society is a society in which power, law and knowledge experience a radical indeterminacy. This is the consequence of the 'democratic revolution', which led to the disappearance of a power that was embodied in the person of the prince and tied to a transcendental authority. A new kind of institution of the social was thereby inaugurated in which power became 'an empty place'.

I think it is vital to stress, as Lefort does, the emergence of a new symbolic framework and the modern impossibility of providing a final guarantee, a definite legitimation. However, instead of simply identifying the modern form of democracy with the empty place of power, I would also want to put emphasis on the distinction between two aspects: on one side, democracy as a form of rule, that is, the principle of the sovereignty of the people; and on the other side, the symbolic framework within which this democratic rule is exercised. The novelty of modern democracy, what makes it properly 'modern', is that, with the advent of the 'democratic revolution', the old democratic principle that 'power should be exercised by the people' emerges again, but this time within a symbolic framework informed by the liberal discourse, with its strong emphasis on the value of individual liberty and on human rights. Those values are central to the liberal tradition and they are constitutive of the modern view of the world. Nevertheless, one should not make them part and parcel of the democratic tradition whose core values, equality and popular sovereignty, are different. Indeed, the separation between church and state, between the realm of the public and that of the private, as well as the very idea of the *Rechtsstaat*, which are central to the politics of liberalism, do not have their origin in the democratic discourse but come from elsewhere.

It is therefore crucial to realize that, with modern democracy, we are dealing with a new political form of society whose specificity comes from the articulation between two different traditions. On one side we have the liberal tradition constituted by the rule of law, the defence of human rights and the respect of individual liberty; on the other the democratic tradition whose main ideas are those of equality, identity between governing and governed and popular sovereignty. There is no necessary relation between those two distinct traditions but only a contingent historical articulation. Through such an articulation, as C. B. MacPherson was keen to emphasize, liberalism was democratized and democracy liberalized. Let's not forget that, while we tend today to take the link between liberalism and democracy for granted, their union, far from being a smooth process, was the result of bitter struggles. Many liberals and many democrats were perfectly aware of the conflict between their respective logics and of the limits that liberal democracy imposed on the realization of their own objectives. Indeed, both sides have constantly tried to interpret its rules in a way that was better suited to their aims. From the theoretical point of view, some liberals like F. A. Hayek have argued that 'democracy [is] essentially a means, an utilitarian device for safeguarding internal peace and individual freedom',[2] useful as long as it did not endanger liberal institutions but to be discarded when it did. Other liberals have followed another strategy, arguing that were the people to decide 'in a rational manner' they could not go against rights and liberties and, if they happened to do so, their verdict should not be accepted as legitimate. From the other side, some democrats have been keen to dismiss liberal institutions as 'bourgeois formal liberties' and to fight for their replacement by direct forms of democracy in which the will of the people could be expressed without hindrances.

The dominant tendency today consists in envisaging democracy in such a way that it is almost exclusively identified with the *Rechtsstaat* and the defence of human rights, leaving aside the element of popular sovereignty, which is deemed to be obsolete. This has created a 'democratic deficit' which, given the central role played by the idea of popular sovereignty in the democratic imaginary, can have very dangerous effects on the allegiance to democratic institutions. The very legitimacy of liberal democracy is based on the idea of popular sovereignty and, as the mobilization of such an idea by right-wing populist politicians indicates, it would be a serious mistake to believe that the time has come to relinquish it. Liberal-democratic institutions should not be taken for granted: it is always necessary to fortify and defend them. This requires grasping their specific dynamics and acknowledging the tension deriving from the workings of their different logics. Only by coming to terms with the democratic paradox can one envisage how to deal with it.

As my discussion of Carl Schmitt's theses in Chapter 2 makes clear, democratic logics always entail drawing a frontier between 'us' and 'them', those who belong to the 'demos' and those who are outside it. This is the condition for the very exercise of democratic rights. It necessarily creates a tension with the liberal emphasis on the respect of 'human rights', since there is no guarantee that a decision made through democratic procedures will not jeopardize some existing rights. In a liberal democracy limits are always put on the exercise of the sovereignty of the people. Those limits are usually presented as providing the very framework for the respect of human rights and as being non-negotiable. In fact, since they depend on the way 'human rights' are defined and interpreted at a given moment, they are the expression of the prevailing hegemony and thereby contestable. What cannot be contestable in a liberal democracy is the idea that it is legitimate to establish limits to popular sovereignty in the name of liberty. Hence its paradoxical nature.

A central argument in this book is that it is vital for democratic politics to understand that liberal democracy results from the articulation of two logics which are incompatible in the last instance and that there is no way in which they could be perfectly reconciled. Or, to put it in a Wittgensteinian way, that there is a constitutive tension between their corresponding 'grammars', a tension that can never be overcome but only negotiated in different ways. This is why the liberal-democratic regime has constantly been the locus of struggles which have provided the driving force of historical political developments. The tension between its two components can only be temporarily stabilized through pragmatic negotiations between political forces which always establish the hegemony of one of them. Until recently, the existence of contending forces was openly recognized and it is only nowadays, when the very idea of a possible alternative to the existing order has been discredited, that the stabilization realized under the hegemony of neo-liberalism – with its very specific interpretation of what rights are important and non-negotiable – is practically unchallenged.

Once it is granted that the tension between equality and liberty cannot be reconciled and that there can only be contingent hegemonic forms of stabilization of their conflict, it becomes clear that, once the very idea of an alternative to the existing configuration of power disappears, what disappears also is the very possibility of a legitimate form of expression for the resistances against the dominant power relations. The status quo has become naturalized and made into the way 'things really are'. This is of course what has happened with the present Zeitgeist, the so-called 'third way', which is no more than the justification by social democrats of their capitulation to a neo-liberal hegemony whose power relations they will not challenge, limiting themselves to making some little adjustments in order to help people cope with what is seen as the ineluctable fate of 'globalization'.

I want to stress that my aim in the essays collected in this volume is at the same time political and theoretical. From the political standpoint what guides me is the conviction that the unchallenged hegemony of neo-liberalism represents a threat for democratic institutions. Neo-liberal dogmas about the unviolable rights of property, the all-encompassing virtues of the market and the dangers of interfering with its logics constitute nowadays the 'common sense' in liberal-democratic societies and they are having a profound impact on the left, as many left parties are moving to the right and euphemistically redefining themselves as 'centre-left'. In a very similar way, Blair's 'third way' and Schröder's 'neue Mitte', both inspired by Clinton's strategy of 'triangulation', accept the terrain established by their neo-liberal predecessors. Unable – or unwilling – to visualize an alternative to the present hegemonic configuration, they advocate a form of politics which pretends to be located 'beyond left and right', categories which are presented as outdated. Their objective is the creation of a 'consensus at the centre', declared to be the only type of politics adapted to the new information society, all those who oppose their 'modernizing' project being dismissed as 'forces of conservatism'. However, as I show in Chapter 5, when we scratch behind their rhetoric, we quickly realize that in fact they have simply given up the traditional struggle of the left for equality. Under the pretence of rethinking and updating democratic demands, their calls for 'modernization', 'flexibility' and 'responsibility' disguise their refusal to consider the demands of the popular sectors which are excluded from their political and societal priorities. Worse even, they are rejected as 'anti-democratic', 'retrograde' and as remnants of a thoroughly discredited 'old left' project. In this increasingly 'one-dimensional' world, in which any possibility of transformation of the relations of power has been erased, it is not surprising that right-wing populist parties are making significant inroads in several countries. In many cases they are the only ones denouncing the 'consensus at the centre' and trying to occupy the terrain of contestation deserted by the left. Particularly worrying is the fact that many sectors of the working classes feel that their interests are better defended by those parties than by social democrats. Having lost faith in the traditional democratic process, they are an easy target for the demagogues of the right.

The political situation just described, characterized by the celebration of the values of a consensual politics of the centre, is what informs my theoretical questioning. This is why I put special emphasis on the negative consequences of envisaging the ideal of democracy as the realization of a 'rational consensus' and on the concomitant illusion that left and right have ceased to be pertinent categories for democratic politics. I am convinced, contrary to the claims of third way theorists, that the blurring of the frontiers between left and right, far from being an advance in a democratic direction, is jeopardizing the future of democracy.

My aim in this volume is to examine in which way political theory could contribute to breaking the current deadlock and to creating some conditions for a possible solution to our present predicament. A significant part of my reflection consists in bringing to the fore the shortcomings of the dominant approach in democratic theory which, I argue, is unable to provide the necessary tools for such an endeavour. In scrutinizing the problems with such an approach I come to the conclusion that the 'consensus model' of democracy which informs both the theories of 'deliberative democracy' and the proposals for a 'third way politics' is unable to grasp the dynamics of modern democratic politics which lies in the confrontation between the two components of the liberal-democratic articulation. In other words, it is the incapacity of democratic theorists and politicians to acknowledge the paradox of which liberal-democratic politics is the expression which is at the origin of their mistaken emphasis on consensus and sustains their belief that antagonism can be eradicated. It is such a failure which impedes the elaboration of an adequate model of democratic politics.[3]

In the field of political theory this is particularly evident in the recent attempts by John Rawls and Jürgen Habermas to reconcile democracy with liberalism which are discussed in Chapter 4. Both authors claim to have found the solution to the problem concerning the compatibility of liberty and equality which has accompanied liberal-democratic thought since its inception. Their solutions are no doubt different, but they share the belief that through adequate deliberative procedures it should be possible to overcome the conflict between individual rights and liberties and the claims for equality and popular participation. According to Habermas such a conflict ceases to exist once one realizes the 'co-originality' of fundamental human rights and of popular sovereignty. However, as I indicate, neither Rawls nor Habermas is able to bring about a satisfactory solution, since each of them ends up by privileging one dimension over the other: liberalism in the case of Rawls, democracy in the case of Habermas. Given the impossibility of an ultimate reconciliation between the two logics which are constitutive of liberal democracy, such a failure was of course to be expected, and it is high time for democratic political theory to abandon this type of sterile search. Only by coming to terms with its paradoxical nature will we be in a position to envisage modern democratic politics in an adequate manner, not as the search for an inaccessible consensus – to be reached through whatever procedure – but as an 'agonistic confrontation' between conflicting interpretations of the constitutive liberal-democratic values. In such a confrontation the left/right configuration plays a crucial role and the illusion that democratic politics could organize itself without them can only have disastrous consequences.

In Chapter 4, I propose to 'redescribe' (to put it in a Rortyan way) liberal democracy in terms of 'agonistic pluralism'. This, I argue, is the best way to acknowledge the tension between its constitutive elements and to harness it in a productive way. I therefore disagree with those who declare that accepting the impossibility of reconciling the two traditions commits us to endorse Carl Schmitt's trenchant verdict about liberal democracy, namely, his thesis that this is a non-viable regime, given that liberalism negates democracy and that democracy negates liberalism. While I consider that Schmitt's critique provides important insights and that it should be taken seriously, my position, developed in Chapter 2, is that this ultimate irreconcilability need not be visualized on the mode of a contradiction but as the locus of a paradox. I state that, while Schmitt is right to highlight the different ways in which the universalistic liberal logic is in opposition to the democratic conception of equality and the need to politically constitute a 'demos', this does not force us to relinquish one of the two traditions. To envisage their articulation as resulting in a paradoxical configuration makes it possible to visualize the tension between the two logics in a positive way, instead of seeing it as leading to a destructive contradiction. Indeed, I suggest that acknowledging this paradox permits us to grasp what is the real strength of liberal democracy.

By constantly challenging the relations of inclusion–exclusion implied by the political constitution of 'the people' – required by the exercise of democracy – the liberal discourse of universal human rights plays an important role in maintaining the democratic contestation alive. On the other side, it is only thanks to the democratic logics of equivalence that frontiers can be created and a demos established without which no real exercise of rights could be possible.

One needs to stress, however, that this tension between democracy and liberalism should not be conceived as one existing between two principles entirely external to each other and establishing between themselves simple relations of negotiation. Were the tension conceived in this way, a very simplistic dualism would have been instituted. The tension should be envisaged instead as creating a relation not of *negotiation* but of *contamination*, in the sense that once the articulation of the two principles has been effectuated – even if in a precarious way – each of them changes the identity of the other. The regimes of collective identities resulting from this process of articulation are ensembles whose configurations are always something more than the addition of their internal elements. As always in social life, there is a 'gestaltic' dimension which is decisive in understanding the perception and behaviour of collective subjects.

Visualizing the dynamics of liberal-democratic politics as the space of a paradox whose effect is to impede both total closure and total dissemination, whose possibility is inscribed in the grammars of democracy and liberalism, opens many interesting possibilities. To be sure, by preventing the full development of their respective logics, this articulation represents an obstacle to their complete realization; both perfect liberty and perfect equality become impossible. But this is the very condition of possibility for a pluralist form of human coexistence in which rights can exist *and* be exercised, in which freedom and equality can somehow manage to coexist. Such an understanding of liberal democracy, however, is precisely what is precluded by the rationalist approach which, instead of acknowledging the ineradicability of this tension, tries to find ways of eliminating it. Hence the need to relinquish the illusion that a rational consensus could ever be achieved where such a tension would be eliminated, and to realize that pluralist democratic politics consists in pragmatic, precarious and necessarily unstable forms of negotiating its constitutive paradox.

This coming to terms with the paradoxical nature of liberal democracy requires breaking with the rationalist dominant perspective and calls for a theoretical framework which acknowledges the impossibility of constituting a form of social objectivity which would not be grounded on an originary exclusion. This is why a continuous thread in my argumentation is to highlight the importance of a non-essentialist approach informed by post-structuralism and deconstruction for a proper understanding of democracy. A key thesis of my work has been for some time that a rationalist approach is bound to remain blind to 'the political' in its dimension of antagonism and that such an omission has very serious consequences for democratic politics. Such a perspective was already introduced in *Hegemony and Socialist Strategy*[4] and in *The Return of the Political*,[5] and several chapters in this book are a continuation of those analyses. In Chapter 3, I also examine what I consider to be Wittgenstein's very important contribution to the elaboration of a non-rationalist approach to political theory. I suggest that we find in the late Wittgenstein many insights which can be used to envisage how allegiance to democratic values is created not through rational argumentation but through an ensemble of language-games which construct democratic forms of individuality. Against the current search – in my view profoundly mistaken – for a legitimacy that would be grounded on rationality, Wittgenstein's view that agreement is reached through participation in common forms of life, as a form of 'Einstimmung' and not of 'Einverstand', represents a path-breaking perspective. Equally important for a truly pluralistic approach is his conception of 'following a rule' which, I argue, can help us with visualizing the diversity of ways in which the democratic game can be played.

The work of Jacques Derrida is also relevant for my project. In his case, it is the notion of the 'constitutive outside' which helps me to emphasize the usefulness of a deconstructive approach in grasping the antagonism inherent in all objectivity and the centrality of the us/them distinction in the constitution of collective political identities. In order to avoid any misunderstanding, let me point out that the 'constitutive outside' cannot be reduced to a dialectical negation. In order to be a true outside, the outside has to be incommensurable with the inside, and at the same time, the condition of emergence of the latter. This is only possible if what is 'outside' is not simply the outside of a concrete content but something which puts into question 'concreteness' as such. This is what is involved in the Derridean notion of the 'constitutive outside': not a content which would be asserted/negated by another content which would just be its dialectical opposite – which would be the case if we were simply saying that there is no 'us' without a 'them' – but a content which, by showing the radical undecidability of the tension of its constitution, makes its very positivity a function of the symbol of something exceeding it: the possibility/impossibility of positivity as such. In this case, antagonism is irreducible to a simple process of dialectical reversal: the 'them' is not the constitutive opposite of a concrete 'us', but the symbol of what makes *any* 'us' impossible.

Understood in that way, the constitutive outside allows us to tackle the conditions of emergence of an antagonism. This arises when this us/them relation, which until then was only perceived as simple difference, began to be seen as one between friend and enemy. From that moment on, it becomes the locus of an antagonism, that is, it becomes political (in Schmitt's sense of the term). If collective identities can only be established on the mode of an us/them, it is clear that, under certain conditions, they can always become transformed into antagonistic relations. Antagonism, then, can never be eliminated and it constitutes an ever-present possibility in politics. A key task of democratic politics is therefore to create the conditions that would make it less likely for such a possibility to emerge.

To see democratic politics from such a perspective is precisely the aim of the project of 'agonistic pluralism' delineated in Chapter 4. A first step in my argumentation is to assert that the friend/enemy opposition is not the only form that antagonism can take and that it can manifest itself in another way. This is why I propose to distinguish between two forms of antagonism, antagonism proper – which takes place between enemies, that is, persons who have no common symbolic space – and what I call 'agonism', which is a different mode of manifestation of antagonism because it involves a relation not between enemies but between 'adversaries', adversaries being defined in a paradoxical way as 'friendly enemies', that is, persons who are friends because they share a common symbolic space but also enemies because they want to organize this common symbolic space in a different way.

I see the category of the 'adversary' as the key to envisage the specificity of modern pluralist democratic politics, and it is at the very centre of my understanding of democracy as 'agonistic pluralism'. Besides allowing me to counter Schmitt's argument about the inconsistency of the idea of pluralist democracy, it helps me to bring to the fore the limitations both of the theorists of 'deliberative democracy' and of the politics of the so-called 'radical centre'. In Chapter 1, for instance, I examine the more recent version of Rawls's political liberalism and show the problematic implications for a pluralist approach of his conception of a 'well-ordered society'. I submit that one of its main shortcomings is precisely that it tends to erase the very place of the adversary, thereby expelling any legitimate opposition from the democratic public sphere.

On the political level a similar phenomenon is to be found in the case of the 'third way' discussed in Chapter 5. I argue that it is a 'politics without adversary' which pretends that all interests can be reconciled and that everybody – provided, of course, that they identify with 'the project' – can be part of 'the people'. In order to justify acceptance of the current neo-liberal hegemony – while pretending to remain radical – the 'third way' mobilizes a view of politics which has evacuated the dimension of antagonism and postulates the existence of a 'general interest of the people' whose implementation overcomes the winners/losers form of resolution of conflicts. The sociological background of such a thesis is that the cycle of confrontational politics that has been dominant in the West since the French Revolution has come to an end. The left/right distinction is now irrelevant, since it was anchored in a social bipolarity that has ceased to exist. For theorists like Anthony Giddens, the left/right divide – which he identifies with old-style social democracy versus market fundamentalism – is an inheritance of 'simple modernization' and has to be transcended. In a globalized world marked by the development of a new individualism, democracy must become 'dialogic'. What we need is a 'life politics' able to reach the various areas of personal life, creating a 'democracy of the emotions'.

What is missing in such a perspective is any grasp of the power relations which structure contemporary post-industrial societies. There is no denying that capitalism has been radically transformed, but this does not mean that its effects have become more benign; far from it. We might have given up the idea of a radical alternative to the capitalist system, but even a renewed and modernized social democracy – which the third way claims to be – will need to challenge the entrenched wealth and power of the new class of managers if it wants to bring about a fairer and more accountable society. The kind of social unanimity which is the trademark of Blairism is only conducive to the maintenance of existing hierarchies. No amount of dialogue or moral preaching will ever convince the ruling class to give up its power. The state cannot limit itself to dealing with the social consequences of market failures.

To be sure, there are many new issues that an emancipatory politics has to tackle. In order to envisage the making of a new hegemony the traditional understanding of left and right needs to be redefined; but whatever the content we give to those categories, one thing is sure: there comes a time when one needs to decide on which side to stand in their agonistic confrontation. What is specific and valuable about modern liberal democracy is that, when properly understood, it creates a space in which this confrontation is kept open, power relations are always being put into question and no victory can be final. However, such an 'agonistic' democracy requires accepting that conflict and division are inherent to politics and that there is no place where reconciliation could be definitively achieved as the full actualization of the unity of 'the people'. To imagine that pluralist democracy could ever be perfectly instantiated is to transform it into a self-refuting ideal, since the condition of possibility of a pluralist democracy is at the same time the condition of impossibility of its perfect implementation. Hence the importance of acknowledging its paradoxical nature.

NOTES

1. Claude Lefort, *Democracy and Political Theory*, Oxford, 1988, p. 19.

2. F. Hayek, *The Road to Serfdom*, London, 1944, p. 52.

3. Once more my reflection dovetails with the work of William Connolly, who – in *Identity/Difference* (Ithaca, 1991) and *The Ethos of Pluralization* (Minneapolis, 1995) – argues for a 'politics of paradox'. While we put the accent on different aspects, since Connolly is particularly interested in bringing to the fore what he calls the 'paradox of difference' and I am specially concerned with the paradox of liberal democracy, our approaches converge on many important points. We both consider that it is vital for a pluralist democratic politics to expose and acknowledge paradoxes instead of trying to conceal or transcend them through appeals to rationality or community.

4. Ernesto Laclau and Chantal Mouffe, *Hegemony and Socialist Strategy: Towards a Radical Democratic Politics*, London, 1985.

5. Chantal Mouffe, *The Return of the Political*, London, 1993.

1

DEMOCRACY, POWER AND 'THE POLITICAL'

In recent decades categories like 'human nature', 'universal reason' and 'rational autonomous subject' have increasingly been put into question. From different standpoints, a variety of thinkers have criticized the ideas of a universal human nature, of a universal canon of rationality through which that human nature could be known, as well as the possibility of an unconditional universal truth. Such a critique of Enlightenment universalism and rationalism – which is sometimes referred to as 'postmodern' – has been presented by some authors, like Jürgen Habermas, as constituting a threat to the modern democratic project. They consider that the link existing between the democratic ideal of the Enlightenment and its rationalistic and universalistic perspective is such that rejecting the latter necessarily jeopardizes the former.

In this chapter I want to take issue with such a view and defend the opposite thesis. Indeed, I am going to argue that it is only in the context of a political theory that takes account of the critique of essentialism – which I see as the crucial contribution of the so-called 'postmodern' approach – that it is possible to formulate the aims of a radical democratic politics in a way that makes room for the contemporary proliferation of political spaces and the multiplicity of democratic demands.[1]

PLURALISM AND MODERN DEMOCRACY

Before developing my argument, I would like to make a few remarks to specify the way I envisage modern liberal democracy. First, I consider that it is important to distinguish liberal democracy from democratic capitalism and to understand it in terms of classical political philosophy as a *regime*, a political form of society that is defined exclusively at the level of the political, leaving aside its possible articulation with an economic system. Liberal democracy – in its various appellations: constitutional democracy, representative democracy, parliamentary democracy, modern democracy – is not the application of the democratic model to a wider context, as some would have it; understood as a *regime* it concerns the symbolic ordering of social relations and is much more than a mere 'form of government'. It is a specific form of organizing politically human coexistence which results from the articulation between two different traditions: on one side, political liberalism (rule of law, separation of powers and individual rights) and, on the other side, the democratic tradition of popular sovereignty.

In other words, the difference between ancient and modern democracy is not one of *size* but of *nature*. The crucial difference resides in the acceptance of *pluralism*, which is constitutive of modern liberal democracy. By 'pluralism' I mean the end of a substantive idea of the good life, what Claude Lefort calls 'the dissolution of the markers of certainty'. Such a recognition of pluralism implies a profound transformation in the symbolic ordering of social relations. This is something that is totally missed when one refers, like John Rawls, to the *fact* of pluralism. There is of course a fact, which is the diversity of the conceptions of the good that we find in a liberal society. But the important difference is not an empirical one; it concerns the *symbolic* level. What is at stake is the legitimation of conflict and division, the emergence of individual liberty and the assertion of equal liberty for all.

Once pluralism is recognized as the defining feature of modern democracy, we can ask what is the best way to approach the scope and nature of a pluralist democratic politics. My contention is that it is only in the context of a perspective according to which 'difference' is construed as the condition of possibility of being that a radical democratic project informed by pluralism can be adequately formulated. Indeed, I submit that all forms of pluralism that depend on a logic of the social that implies the idea of 'being as presence', and sees 'objectivity' as belonging to the 'things themselves', necessarily lead to the reduction of plurality and to its ultimate negation. This is indeed the case with the main forms of liberal pluralism, which generally start by stressing what they call 'the fact of pluralism', and then go on to find procedures to deal with differences whose objective is actually to make those differences irrelevant and to relegate pluralism to the sphere of the private.

Envisaged from an anti-essentialist theoretical perspective, on the contrary, pluralism is not merely a *fact*, something that we must bear grudgingly or try to reduce, but an axiological principle. It is taken to be constitutive *at the conceptual level* of the very nature of modern democracy and considered as something that we should celebrate and enhance. This is why the type of pluralism that I am advocating gives a positive status to differences and questions the objective of unanimity and homogeneity, which is always revealed as fictitious and based on acts of exclusion.

However, such a view does not allow a total pluralism and it is important to recognize the limits to pluralism which are required by a democratic politics that aims at challenging a wide range of relations of subordination. It is therefore necessary to distinguish the position I am defending here from the type of extreme pluralism that emphasizes heterogeneity and incommensurability and according to which pluralism – understood as valorization of all differences – should have no limits. I consider that, despite its claim to be more democratic, such a perspective prevents us from recognizing how certain differences are constructed as relations of subordination and should therefore be challenged by a radical democratic politics. There is only a multiplicity of identities without any common denominator, and it is impossible to distinguish between differences that exist but should not exist and differences that do not exist but should exist.

What such a pluralism misses is the dimension of the *political*. Relations of power and antagonisms are erased and we are left with the typical liberal illusion of a pluralism without antagonism. Indeed, although it tends to be very critical of liberalism, that type of extreme pluralism, because of its refusal of any attempt to construct a 'we', a collective identity that would articulate the demands found in the different struggles against subordination, partakes of the liberal evasion of the political. To deny the need for a construction of such collective identities, and to conceive democratic politics exclusively in terms of a struggle of a multiplicity of interest groups or of minorities for the assertion of their rights, is to remain blind to the relations of power. It is to ignore the limits imposed on the extension of the sphere of rights by the fact that some existing rights have been constructed on the very exclusion or subordination of others.

PLURALISM, POWER AND ANTAGONISM

In coming to terms with pluralism, what is really at stake is power and antagonism and their ineradicable character. This can only be grasped from a perspective that puts into question the objectivism and essentialism which are dominant in democratic theory. In *Hegemony and Socialist Strategy*,[2] we delineated an approach that asserts that any social objectivity is constituted through acts of power. This means that any social objectivity is ultimately political and has to show the traces of the acts of exclusion which govern its constitution; what, following Derrida, can be referred to as its 'constitutive outside'.

This point is decisive. It is because every object has inscribed in its very being something other than itself and that as a result, everything is constructed as *difference*, that its being cannot be conceived as pure 'presence' or 'objectivity'. Since the constitutive outside is present within the inside as its always real possibility, every identity becomes purely contingent. This implies that we should not conceptualize power as an *external* relation taking place between two pre-constituted identities, but rather as constituting the identities themselves. This point of confluence between objectivity and power is what we have called 'hegemony'.

When we envisage democratic politics from such an anti-essentialist perspective, we can begin to undestand that, for democracy to exist, no social agent should be able to claim any mastery of the *foundation* of society. This signifies that the relation between social agents becomes more democratic only as far as they accept the particularity and the limitation of their claims; that is, only in so far as they recognize their mutual relation as one from which power is ineradicable. The democratic society cannot be conceived any more as a society that would have realized the dream of a perfect harmony in social relations. Its democratic character can only be given by the fact that no limited social actor can attribute to herself or himself the representation of the totality. The main question of democratic politics becomes then not how to eliminate power, but how to constitute forms of power which are compatible with democratic values.

To acknowledge the existence of relations of power and the need to transform them, while renouncing the illusion that we could free ourselves completely from power – this is what is specific to the project that we have called 'radical and plural democracy'. Such a project recognizes that the specificity of modern pluralist democracy – even a well-ordered one – does not reside in the absence of domination and of violence but in the establishment of a set of institutions through which they can be limited and contested. To negate the ineradicable character of antagonism and to aim at a universal rational consensus – this is the real threat to democracy. Indeed, this can lead to violence being unrecognized and hidden behind appeals to 'rationality', as is often the case in liberal thinking which disguises the necessary frontiers and forms of exclusion behind pretences of 'neutrality'.

POLITICAL LIBERALISM

To illustrate the dangerous consequences of the rationalist approach and show the superiority of the one I am delineating here, I have chosen to take the example of the 'political liberalism' of John Rawls. In his recent work, Rawls intends to give a new solution to the traditional liberal problem of how to

establish peaceful coexistence among people with different conceptions of the good. For a long time liberals have seen the
solution to that problem in the creation of a modus vivendi or,
following Schumpeter, a 'modus procedendi' that regulates the
conflict among different views. Hence the generally accepted
view of democracy as a procedural form, neutral with respect to
any particular set of values, a mere method for making public
decisions.

Recently, liberals like Rawls – and in a slightly different way
Charles Larmore – have taken issue with such an interpretation
of the liberal principle of neutrality. They affirm that a liberal-
democratic society needs a form of consensus that is deeper than
a simple modus vivendi on mere procedures. Its aim should be
the creation of a moral and not only prudential type of consensus
around its basic institutions. Their objective is to provide a
moral, albeit minimal, consensus on political fundamentals.
Their 'political liberalism' aims at defining a core morality that
specifies the terms under which people with different conceptions of the good can live together in political association. It is
an understanding of liberalism which is compatible with the fact
of pluralism and the existence of moral and religious disagreement, and must be distinguished from comprehensive views like
those of Kant and Mill. Given that it is neutral with respect to
controversial views of the good life, they believe that such a
liberalism can provide the political principles that should be
accepted by all despite their differences.[3]

According to Rawls, the problem of political liberalism can be
formulated in the following way: 'How is it possible that there
may exist over time a stable and just society of free and equal
citizens profoundly divided by reasonable religious, philosophical
and moral doctrines?'[4] The problem, in his view, is one of

political *justice*, and it requires the establishment of fair terms of social co-operation between citizens envisaged as free and equal, but also as divided by profound doctrinal conflict. His solution, as reformulated in his book *Political Liberalism*, puts a new emphasis on the notion of 'reasonable pluralism'. He invites us to distinguish between what would be a mere empirical recognition of opposed conceptions of the good, the fact of 'simple' pluralism, and what is the real problem facing liberals: how to deal with a plurality of incompatible yet *reasonable* doctrines. He sees such a plurality as the normal result of the exercise of human reason within the framework of a constitutional democratic regime. This is why a conception of justice must be able to gain the support of all 'reasonable' citizens, despite their deep doctrinal disagreements on other matters.

Let's examine this distinction between 'simple' and 'reasonable' pluralism. Avowedly it is supposed to secure the moral character of the consensus on justice which precludes that a compromise should be made with 'unreasonable' views; that is, those which would oppose the basic principles of political morality. But in fact, it allows Rawls to present as a moral exigency what is really a political decision. For Rawls, reasonable persons are persons 'who have realized their two moral powers to a degree sufficient to be free and equal citizens in a constitutional regime, and who have an enduring desire to honor fair terms of cooperation and to be fully cooperating members of society'.[5]

What is this if not an indirect form of asserting that reasonable persons are those who accept the fundamentals of liberalism? In other words, the distinction between 'reasonable' and 'unreasonable' helps to draw a frontier between the doctrines that accept the liberal principles and the ones that oppose them.

It means that its function is *political* and that it aims at discriminating between a permissible pluralism of religious, moral or philosophical conceptions, as long as those views can be relegated to the sphere of the private and satisfy the liberal principles – and what would be an unacceptable pluralism because it would jeopardize the dominance of liberal principles in the public sphere.

What Rawls is really indicating with such a distinction is that there cannot be pluralism as far as the principles of the political association are concerned, and that conceptions which refuse the principles of liberalism are to be excluded. I have no quarrel with him on this issue. But this is the expression of an eminently *political* decision, not of a moral requirement. To call the anti-liberals 'unreasonable' is a way of stating that such views cannot be admitted as legitimate within the framework of a liberal-democratic regime. This is indeed the case, but the reason for such an exclusion is not a moral one. It is because antagonistic principles of legitimacy cannot coexist within the same political association without putting in question the political reality of the state. However, to be properly formulated, such a thesis calls for a theoretical framework that asserts that the political is always constitutive – which is precisely what liberalism denies.

Rawls tries to avoid the problem by presenting his priority of the right over the good as a moral distinction. But that does not solve the problem. First, a question arises concerning the status of his assertion of the priority of the right over the good. To be consistent Rawls cannot derive it from any comprehensive doctrine. Is it, then, only an 'intuitive idea' that we all share? The communitarians would certainly object to such a view. So, what can it be? The answer is, of course, that it is one of the main features of liberal democracy understood as a distinctive political form of society; it is part of the 'grammar' of such a 'regime'. But an answer on those lines is not available to Rawls because there is no place for such a constitutive role of the political in his theory. This is why he cannot provide a convincing argument for justifying the frontiers of his pluralism, and why he gets caught in a circular form of argumentation: political liberalism can provide a consensus among reasonable persons who, *by definition*, are persons who accept the principles of political liberalism.

OVERLAPPING CONSENSUS OR CONSTITUTIONAL CONSENSUS

Another consequence of Rawls's incapacity to apprehend the constitutive role of the political is revealed when we scrutinize another aspect of his solution to the liberal problem: the creation of an 'overlapping consensus' of reasonable comprehensive doctrines in which each of them endorses the political conception from its own point of view. He declares that when a society is well-ordered, it is around the principles of his theory of justice as fairness that the overlapping consensus is established. Since they are chosen thanks to the device of the original position with its 'veil of ignorance', those principles of fair terms of co-operation satisfy the liberal principle of legitimacy that requires that they are endorsed by all citizens as free and equal – as well as reasonable and rational – and addressed to their public reason. According to the standpoint of political liberalism, those principles are expressly designed to gain the reasoned support of citizens who affirm reasonable though conflicting comprehensive doctrines. Indeed, the very purpose of the veil of ignorance is to preclude the knowledge of citizens' comprehensive conceptions of the good and to force them to proceed from the shared conceptions of society and person required in applying the ideals and principles of practical reason.[6]

In line with his project of establishing the moral character of his 'political liberalism', Rawls is at pains to indicate that such an overlapping consensus must not be confused with a simple modus vivendi. He insists that it is not merely a consensus on a set of institutional arrangements based on self-interest but the affirmation on moral grounds of principles of justice that have themselves a moral character. Moreover, the overlapping consensus also differs from a constitutional form of consensus which, in his view, is not deep or wide enough to secure justice and stability. In a constitutional consensus, he states:

> while there is agreement on certain basic political rights and liberties – on the right to vote and freedom of political speech and association, and whatever else is required for the electoral and legislative procedures of democracy – there is disagreement among those holding liberal principles as to the more exact content and boundaries of these rights and liberties, as well as on what further rights and liberties are to be counted as basic and so merit legal if not constitutional protection.[7]

Rawls grants that a constitutional consensus is better than a modus vivendi because there is a real allegiance to the principles of a liberal constitution that guarantee certain basic rights and liberties and establish democratic procedures for moderating political rivalry. Nevertheless, given that those principles are not grounded in certain ideas of society and person of a political conception, disagreements subsist concerning the status and content of those rights and liberties, and they create insecurity and hostility in public life. Hence, he says, the importance of fixing their content *once and for all*. This is provided by an overlapping consensus on a conception of justice as fairness, which establishes a much deeper consensus than one that would be restricted to constitutional essentials. While admitting that those constitutional essentials (namely, fundamental principles that specify the general structure of government and the political process as well as basic rights and liberties of citizenship)[8] are more urgent to settle, Rawls considers that they must be distinguished from the principles governing social and economic inequalities. The aim of justice as fairness is to establish a consensus on a public reason whose content is given by a political conception of justice: 'this content has two parts: substantive principles of justice for the basic structure (the political values of justice); and guidelines of enquiry and conceptions of virtue that make public reason possible (the political values of public reason)'.[9]

Rawls seems to believe that whereas rational agreement among comprehensive moral religious and philosophical doctrine is impossible, in the political domain such an agreement can be reached. Once the controversial doctrines have been relegated to the sphere of the private, it is possible, in his view, to establish in the public sphere a type of consensus grounded on Reason (with its two sides: the rational and the reasonable). This is a consensus that it would be illegitimate to put into question once it has been reached, and the only possibility of destabilization would be an attack from the outside by the 'unreasonable' forces. This implies that when a well-ordered society has been achieved, those who take part in the overlapping consensus should have no right to question the existing arrangements, since they embody the principles of justice. If somebody does not comply, it must be due to 'irrationality' or 'unreasonableness'.

At this point, the picture of the Rawlsian well-ordered society begins to emerge more clearly and it looks very much like a dangerous utopia of reconciliation. To be sure, Rawls recognizes that a full overlapping consensus might never be achieved but at best approximated. It is more likely, he says, that the focus of an overlapping consensus will be a class of liberal conceptions acting as political rivals.[10] Nevertheless, he urges us to strive for a well-ordered society where, given that there is no more conflict between political and economic interests, this rivalry has been overcome. Such a society would see the realization of justice as fairness, which is the correct and definite interpretation of how the democratic principles of equality and liberty should be implemented in the basic institutions. It is independent of any interest, does not represent any form of compromise, but is truly the expression of free public democratic reason.

The way he envisages the nature of the overlapping consensus clearly indicates that, for Rawls, a well-ordered society is a society from which politics has been eliminated. A conception of justice is mutually recognized by reasonable and rational citizens who act according to its injunctions. They probably have very different and even conflicting conceptions of the good, but those are strictly private matters and they do not interfere with their public life. Conflicts of interest about economic and social issues – if they still arise – are resolved smoothly through discussions within the framework of public reason, by invoking the principles of justice that everybody endorses. If an unreasonable or irrational person happens to disagree with that state of affairs and intends to disrupt that nice consensus, she or he must be forced, through coercion, to submit to the principles of justice. Such a coercion, however, has nothing to do with oppression, since it is justified by the exercise of reason.

What Rawls's view of the well-ordered society eliminates is the democratic struggle among 'adversaries', that is, those who share the allegiance to the liberal-democratic principles, but while defending different interpretations of what liberty and equality should mean and to which kind of social relations and institutions they should apply. This is why in his 'liberal utopia' legitimate dissent would have been eradicated from the public sphere. How has he been led to defend such a position? Why doesn't his conception of democracy leave any space for the agonistic confrontation among contested interpretations of the shared liberal-democratic principles? The answer lies, I believe, in his flawed conception of politics, which is reduced to a mere activity of allocating among competing interests susceptible to a rational solution. This is why he thinks that political conflicts can be eliminated thanks to a conception of justice that appeals to individuals' idea of rational advantage within the constraints established by the reasonable.

According to his theory, citizens need as free and equal persons the same goods because their conceptions of the good – however distinct their content – 'require for their advancement roughly the same primary goods, that is, the same basic rights, liberties, and opportunities, and the same all-purpose means such as income and wealth, with all of these supported by the same social bases of self-respect'.[11] Therefore, once the just answer to the problem of distribution of those primary goods has been found, the rivalry that previously existed in the political domain disappears.

Rawls's scenario presupposes that political actors are only driven by what they see as their rational self-advantage. Passions are erased from the realm of politics, which is reduced to a neutral field of competing interests. Completely missing from such an approach is 'the political' in its dimension of power, antagonism and relationships of forces. What 'political liberalism' is at pains to eliminate is the element of 'undecidability' which is present in human relations. It offers us a picture of the well-ordered society as one from which – through rational agreement on justice – antagonism, violence, power and repression have disappeared. But it is only because they have been made invisible through a clever stratagem: the distinction between 'simple' and 'reasonable pluralism'. In that way, exclusions can be denied by declaring that they are the product of the 'free exercise of practical reason' that establishes the limits of possible consensus. When a point of view is excluded it is because this is required by the exercise of reason; therefore the frontiers between what is legitimate and what is not legitimate appear as independent of power relations. Thanks to this legerdemain, rationality and morality provide the key to solving the 'paradox of liberalism': how to eliminate its adversaries while remaining neutral.

Alas, it is not enough to eliminate the political in its dimension of antagonism and exclusion from one's theory to make it vanish from the real world. It does come back, and with a vengeance. Once the liberal approach has created a framework in which its dynamics cannot be grasped, and where the institutions and the discourses are missing that could permit that potential antagonisms manifest themselves under an agonistic mode, the danger exists that instead of a struggle among adversaries, what will take place is a war between enemies. This is why, far from being conducive to a more reconciled society, this type of approach ends up by jeopardizing democracy.

DEMOCRACY AND UNDECIDABILITY

By bringing to light the potential consequences of Rawls's project, my aim was to reveal the danger of postulating that there could be a rational definite solution to the question of justice in a democratic society. Such an idea leads to the closing of the gap between justice and law that is a constitutive space of modern democracy. To avoid such a closure, we should relinquish the very idea that there could be such a thing as a 'rational' political consensus; namely, one that would not be based on any form of exclusion. To present the institutions of liberal democracy as the outcome of a pure deliberative rationality is to reify them and make them impossible to transform. It is to deny the fact that, like any other regime, modern pluralist democracy constitutes a system of relations of power, and to render the democratic challenging of those forms of power illegitimate.

To believe that a final resolution of conflicts is eventually possible – even if it is seen as an asymptotic approach to the regulative idea of a rational consensus – far from providing the necessary horizon of the democratic project, is something that puts it at risk. Indeed, such an illusion carries implicitly the desire for a reconciled society where pluralism would have been superseded. When it is conceived in such a way, pluralist democracy becomes a 'self-refuting ideal' because the very moment of its realization would coincide with its disintegration.

With its insistence on the irreducible alterity that represents both a condition of possibility and a condition of impossibility of every identity, a perspective informed by post-structuralism provides a much better theoretical framework to grasp the specificity of modern democracy than rationalist approaches. The notion of the 'constitutive outside' forces us to come to terms with the idea that pluralism implies the permanence of conflict and antagonism. Indeed, it helps us to understand that conflict and division are not to be seen as disturbances that unfortunately cannot be completely eliminated, or as empirical impediments that render impossible the full realization of a good constituted by a harmony that we cannot reach because we will never be completely able to coincide with our rational universal self.

Thanks to the insights of post-structuralism the project of radical and plural democracy is able to acknowledge that difference is the condition of the possibility of constituting unity and totality at the same time that it provides their essential limits. In such a view, plurality cannot be eliminated; it becomes irreducible. We have therefore to abandon the very idea of a complete reabsorption of alterity into oneness and harmony. It is an alterity that cannot be domesticated, but as Rodolphe Gasché indicates: 'forever undermines, but also makes possible, the dream of autonomy achieved through a reflexive coiling upon self, since it names the precondition of such a desired state, a precondition that represents the limit of such a possibility'.[12]

Contrary to other projects of radical or participatory democracy informed by a rationalistic framework, radical and plural democracy rejects the very possibility of a non-exclusive public sphere of rational argument where a non-coercive consensus could be attained. By showing that such a consensus is a *conceptual* impossibility, it does not put in jeopardy the democratic ideal, as some would argue. On the contrary, it protects pluralist democracy against any attempts at closure. Indeed, such a rejection constitutes an important guarantee that the dynamics of the democratic process will be kept alive.

Instead of trying to erase the traces of power and exclusion, democratic politics requires us to bring them to the fore, to make them visible so that they can enter the terrain of contestation. And the fact that this must be envisaged as an unending process should not be cause for despair because the desire to reach a final destination can only lead to the elimination of the political and to the destruction of democracy. In a democratic polity, conflicts and confrontations, far from being a sign of imperfection, indicate that democracy is alive and inhabited by pluralism.

To the Kantian-inspired model of democracy which envisages its realization under the form of an ideal community of communication, as a task conceived as infinite, to be sure, but which has nevertheless a clearly defined shape, we should oppose a conception of democracy that, far from aiming at consensus and transparency, is suspicious of any attempt to impose a univocal model of democratic discussion. Aware of the dangers of rationalism, this is a view that does not dream of mastering or eliminating undecidability, for it recognizes that it is the very condition of possibility of decision and therefore of freedom and pluralism.

NOTES

1. I have on several occasions pointed out to the disingenuous a move that consists in conflating post-structuralism with postmodernism, and I will not repeat this argument here. Let's just recall that the anti-essentialism that I am endorsing, far from being restricted to post-structuralism, constitutes the point of convergence of many different currents of thought and that it can be found in authors as different as Derrida, Rorty, Wittgenstein, Heidegger, Gadamer, Dewey, Lacan and Foucault.

2. Ernesto Laclau and Chantal Mouffe, *Hegemony and Socialist Strategy: Towards a Radical Democratic Politics*, London, 1985.

3. For a critique of this attempt by Larmore and Rawls to reformulate the

liberal notion of neutrality, see Chantal Mouffe, *The Return of the Political*, London, 1993, Chapter 9.

4. John Rawls, *Political Liberalism*, New York, 1993, p. xviii.

5. Ibid., p. 55.

6. Ibid., p. 141.

7. Ibid., p. 159.

8. Ibid., p. 227.

9. Ibid., p. 253.

10. Ibid., p. 164.

11. Ibid., p. 180.

12. Rodolphe Gasché, *The Tain of the Mirror*, Cambridge, MA, 1986, p. 105.

2

CARL SCHMITT AND THE PARADOX
OF LIBERAL DEMOCRACY

In his introduction to the paperback edition of *Political Liberal-ism*, John Rawls, referring to Carl Schmitt's critique of parliamentary democracy, suggests that the fall of Weimar's constitutional regime was in part due to the fact that German elites no longer believed in the possibility of a decent liberal parliamentary regime. In his view, this should make us realize the importance of providing convincing arguments in favour of a just and well-ordered constitutional democracy. 'Debates about general philosophical questions', he says, 'cannot be the daily stuff of politics, but that does not make these questions without significance, since what we think their answers are will shape the underlying attitudes of the public culture and the conduct of politics.'[1]

I agree with Rawls on the practical role that political philosophy can play in shaping the public culture and contributing to the creation of democratic political identities. But I consider that political theorists, in order to put forward a conception of a liberal-democratic society able to win the active support of its citizens, must be willing to engage with the arguments of those who have challenged the fundamental tenets of liberalism. This means confronting some disturbing questions, usually avoided by liberals and democrats alike.

My intention in this chapter is to contribute to such a project by scrutinizing Carl Schmitt's critique of liberal democracy. Indeed, I am convinced that a confrontation with his thought will allow us to acknowledge – and, therefore, be in a better position to try to negotiate – an important paradox inscribed in the very nature of liberal democracy. To bring to the fore the pertinence and actuality of Schmitt's questioning, I will organize my argument around two topics which are currently central in political theory: the boundaries of citizenship and the nature of a liberal-democratic consensus.[2]

DEMOCRACY, HOMOGENEITY AND THE BOUNDARIES OF CITIZENSHIP

The boundaries of citizenship have recently provoked much discussion. Several authors have argued that in an age of globalization, citizenship cannot be confined within the boundaries of nation-states; it must become transnational. David Held, for instance, advocates the advent of a 'cosmopolitan citizenship', and asserts the need for a cosmopolitan democratic law to which citizens whose rights have been violated by their own states could appeal.[3] Richard Falk, for his part, envisages the development of 'citizen pilgrims' whose loyalties would belong to an invisible political community of their hopes and dreams.[4]

Other theorists, however, particularly those who are committed to a civic republican conception of citizenship, are deeply suspicious of such prospects, which they view as endangering democratic forms of government. They assert that the nation-state is the necessary locus for citizenship, and that there is something inherently contradictory in the very idea of cosmopolitan citizenship. I see this debate as a typical example of the problems arising from the conflict between democratic and liberal requirements. Schmitt, I submit, can help us to clarify what is at stake in this issue by making us aware of the tension between democracy and liberalism.

As a starting point, let us take his thesis that 'homogeneity' is a condition of possibility of democracy. In the preface to the second edition of *The Crisis of Parliamentary Democracy* (1926), he declares: 'Every actual democracy rests on the principle that not only are equals equal but unequals will not be treated equally. Democracy requires, therefore, first homogeneity and second – if the need arises – elimination or eradication of heterogeneity.'[5] I do not want to deny that, given its author's later political evolution, this assertion has a chilling effect. I consider, however, that it would be short-sighted to dismiss Schmitt's claim on the necessity of homogeneity in a democracy for that reason. It is my contention that this provocative thesis – interpreted in a certain way – may force us to come to terms with an aspect of democratic politics that liberalism tends to eliminate.

The first thing to do is to grasp what Schmitt means by 'homogeneity'. He affirms that homogeneity is inscribed at the very core of the democratic conception of equality, in so far as it must be a *substantive* equality. His argument is that democracy requires a conception of equality as substance, and cannot satisfy itself with abstract conceptions like the liberal one, since 'equality is only interesting and invaluable politically so long as it has substance, and for that reason at least the possibility and the risk of inequality'.[6] In order to be treated as equals, citizens must, he says, partake of a common substance.

As a consequence, he rejects the idea that the general equality of mankind could serve as a basis for a state or any form of government. Such an idea of human equality – which comes from liberal individualism – is, says Schmitt, a non-political form of equality, because it lacks the correlate of a possible inequality from which every equality receives its specific meaning. It does not provide any criteria for establishing political institutions: 'The equality of all persons as persons is not democracy but a certain kind of liberalism, not a state form but an individualistic-humanitarian ethic and *Weltanschauung*. Modern mass democracy rests on the confused combination of both.'[7]

Schmitt asserts that there is an insuperable opposition between liberal individualism, with its moral discourse centred around the individual, and the democratic ideal, which is essentially political, and aims at creating an identity based on homogeneity. He claims that liberalism negates democracy and democracy negates liberalism, and that parliamentary democracy, since it consists in the articulation between democracy and liberalism, is therefore a non-viable regime.

In his view, when we speak of equality, we need to distinguish between two very different ideas: the liberal one and the democratic one. The liberal conception of equality postulates that every person is, as a person, automatically equal to every other person. The democratic conception, however, requires the possibility of distinguishing who belongs to the demos and who is exterior to it; for that reason, it cannot exist without the necessary correlate of inequality. Despite liberal claims, a democracy of mankind, if it was ever likely, would be a pure abstraction, because equality can exist only through its specific meanings in particular spheres – as political equality, economic equality, and so forth. But those specific equalities always entail, as their very condition of possibility, some form of inequality.

This is why he concludes that an absolute human equality would be a practically meaningless, indifferent equality.

Schmitt makes an important point when he stresses that the democratic concept of equality is a *political* one which therefore entails the possibility of a *distinction*. He is right to say that a political democracy cannot be based on the generality of all mankind, and that it must belong to a specific people. It is worth indicating in this context that – contrary to several tendentious interpretations – he never postulated that this belonging to a people could be envisaged only in racial terms. On the contrary, he insisted on the multiplicity of ways in which the homogeneity constitutive of a demos could be manifested. He says, for instance, that the substance of equality 'can be found in certain physical and moral qualities, for example, in civic virtue, in arete, the classical democracy of vertus [vertu]'.[8] Examining this question from a historical angle, he also points out that 'In the democracy of English sects during the seventeenth century equality was based on a consensus of religious convictions. However, since the nineteenth century it has existed above all in membership in a particular nation, in national homogeneity.'[9]

It is clear that what is important for Schmitt is not the nature of the similarity on which homogeneity is based. What matters is the possibility of tracing a line of demarcation between those who belong to the demos – and therefore have equal rights – and those who, in the political domain, cannot have the same rights because they are not part of the demos. Such a democratic equality – expressed today through citizenship – is, for him, the ground of all the other forms of equality. It is through their belonging to the demos that democratic citizens are granted equal rights, not because they participate in an abstract idea of humanity. This is why he declares that the central concept of democracy is not 'humanity' but the concept of the 'people', and that there can never be a democracy of mankind. Democracy can exist only for a people. As he puts it:

In the domain of the political, people do not face each other as abstractions but as politically interested and politically determined persons, as citizens, governors or governed, politically allied or opponents – in any case, therefore, in political categories. In the sphere of the political, one cannot abstract out what is political, leaving only universal human equality.[10]

In order to illustrate his point, Schmitt indicates that even in modern democratic states, where a universal human equality has been established, there is a category of people who are excluded as foreigners or aliens, and that there is therefore no absolute equality of persons. He also shows how the correlate of the equality among the citizenry found in those states is a much stronger emphasis on national homogeneity, and on the line of demarcation between those who belong to the state and those who remain outside it. This, he notes, is to be expected, and if it were not the case, and if a state attempted to realize the universal equality of individuals in the political realm without concern for national or any other form of homogeneity, the consequence would be a complete devaluation of political equality, and of politics itself. To be sure, this would in no way mean the disappearance of substantive inequalities, but, says Schmitt:

they would shift into another sphere, perhaps separated from the political and concentrated in the economic, leaving this area to take on a new, disproportionately decisive importance.

Under the conditions of superficial political equality, another sphere in which substantial inequalities prevail (today for example the economic sphere) will dominate politics.[11]

It seems to me that, unpleasant as they are to liberal ears, these arguments need to be considered carefully. They carry an important warning for those who believe that the process of globalization is laying the basis for worldwide democratization and the establishment of a cosmopolitan citizenship. They also provide important insights into the current dominance of economics over politics. We should indeed be aware that without a demos to which they belong, those cosmopolitan citizen pilgrims would in fact have lost the possibility of exercising their democratic rights of law-making. They would be left, at best, with their liberal rights of appealing to transnational courts to defend their individual rights when these have been violated. In all probability, such a cosmopolitan democracy, if it were ever to be realized, would be no more than an empty name disguising the actual disappearance of democratic forms of government and indicating the triumph of the liberal form of governmental rationality.

THE DEMOCRATIC LOGIC OF INCLUSION-EXCLUSION

It is true that by reading him in this way, I am doing violence to Schmitt's questioning, since his main concern is not democratic participation but *political unity*. He considers that such a unity is crucial, because without it the state cannot exist. But his reflections are relevant to the issue of democracy, since he considers that in a democratic state, it is through their participation in this unity that citizens can be treated as equals and exercise their democratic rights. Democracy, according to Schmitt, consists fundamentally in the identity between rulers and ruled. It is linked to the fundamental principle of the unity of the demos and the sovereignty of its will. But if the people are to rule, it is necessary to determine who belongs to the people. Without any criterion to determine who are the bearers of democratic rights, the will of the people could never take shape.

It could, of course, be objected that this is a view of democracy which is at odds with the liberal-democratic one, and some would certainly claim that this should be called not democracy but populism. To be sure, Schmitt is no democrat in the liberal understanding of the term, and he had nothing but contempt for the constraints imposed by liberal institutions on the democratic will of the people. But the issue he raises is a crucial one, even for those who advocate liberal-democratic forms. The logic of democracy does indeed imply a moment of closure which is required by the very process of constituting the 'people'. This cannot be avoided, even in a liberal-democratic model; it can only be negotiated differently. But this in turn can be done only if this closure, and the paradox it implies, are acknowledged.

By stressing that the identity of a democratic political community hinges on the possibility of drawing a frontier between 'us' and 'them', Schmitt highlights the fact that democracy always entails relations of inclusion–exclusion. This is a vital insight that democrats would be ill-advised to dismiss because they dislike its author. One of the main problems with liberalism – and one that can endanger democracy – is precisely its incapacity to conceptualize such a frontier. As Schmitt indicates, the central concept of liberal discourse is 'humanity', which – as he rightly points out – is not a political concept, and does not correspond to any political entity. The central question of the political constitution of 'the people' is something that liberal theory is unable to tackle adequately, because the necessity of drawing such a 'frontier' contradicts its universalistic rhetoric. Against the liberal emphasis on 'humanity', it is important to stress that the key concepts of democracy are the 'demos' and the 'people'.

Contrary to those who believe in a necessary harmony between liberalism and democracy, Schmitt makes us see how they conflict, and the dangers the dominance of liberal logic can bring to the exercise of democracy. No doubt there is an opposition between the liberal 'grammar' of equality, which postulates universality and reference to 'humanity', and the practice of democratic equality, which requires the political moment of discrimination between 'us' and 'them'. However, I think that Schmitt is wrong to present this conflict as a contradiction that is bound to lead liberal democracy to self-destruction. We can accept his insight perfectly well without agreeing with the conclusions he draws. I propose to acknowledge the crucial difference between the liberal and the democratic conceptions of equality, while envisaging their articulation and its consequences in another way. Indeed, such an articulation can be seen as the locus of a *tension* that installs a very important dynamic, which is constitutive of the specificity of liberal democracy as a new political form of society. The democratic logic of constituting the people, and inscribing rights and equality into practices, is necessary to subvert the tendency towards abstract universalism inherent in liberal discourse. But the articulation with the liberal logic allows us constantly to challenge – through reference to 'humanity' and the polemical use of 'human rights' – the forms of exclusion that are necessarily inscribed in the political practice of installing those rights and defining 'the people' which is going to rule.[12] Notwithstanding the ultimate contradictory nature of the two logics, their articulation therefore has very positive consequences, and there is no reason to share Schmitt's pessimistic verdict concerning liberal democracy. However, we should not be too sanguine about its prospect either. No final resolution or equilibrium between those two conflicting logics is ever possible, and there can be only temporary, pragmatic, unstable and precarious negotiations of the tension between them. Liberal-democratic politics consists, in fact, in the constant process of negotiation and renegotiation – through different hegemonic articulations – of this constitutive paradox.

DELIBERATIVE DEMOCRACY AND ITS SHORTCOMINGS

Schmitt's reflections on the necessary moment of closure entailed by the democratic logic have important consequences for another debate, the one about the nature of the consensus that can obtain in a liberal-democratic society. Several issues are at stake in that debate, and I will examine them in turn.

One of the implications of the argument presented above is the impossibility of establishing a rational consensus without exclusion. This raises several problems for the model of democratic politics, which has been receiving quite a lot of attention recently under the name 'deliberative democracy'. No doubt, the aim of the theorists who advocate the different versions of such a model is commendable. Against the interest-based conception of democracy, inspired by economics and sceptical about the virtues of political participation, they want to introduce questions of morality and justice into politics, and envisage democratic citizenship in a different way. However, by proposing to view reason and rational argumentation, rather than interest and aggregation of preferences, as the central issue of politics, they simply replace the economic model with a moral one which – albeit in a different way – also misses the specificity of the political. In their attempt to overcome the limitations of interest-group pluralism, deliberative democrats provide a telling illustration of Schmitt's point that 'In a very systematic fashion liberal thought evades or ignores state and politics and moves instead in a typical, always recurring polarity of two heterogeneous spheres, namely ethics and economics, intellect and trade, education and property.'[13]

Since I cannot examine all the different versions of deliberative democracy here, I will concentrate on the model developed by Habermas and his followers. To be sure, there are several differences among the advocates of this new paradigm. But there is enough convergence among them to affirm that none of them can deal adequately with the paradox of democratic politics.[14]

According to Seyla Benhabib, the main challenge confronting democracy is how to reconcile rationality with legitimacy – or, to put it differently, the crucial question that democracy needs to address is how the expression of the common good can be made compatible with the sovereignty of the people. She presents the answer offered by the deliberative model:

legitimacy and rationality can be attained with regard to collective decision-making processes in a polity if and only if the institutions of this polity and their interlocking relationship are so arranged that what is considered in the common interest of all results from processes of collective deliberation conducted rationally and fairly among free and equal individuals.[15]

In this view, the basis of legitimacy in democratic institutions derives from the fact that those who claim obligatory power do so on the presumption that their decisions represent an *impartial standpoint* which is *equally in the interests of all*. If this presumption is to be fulfilled, those decisions must be the result of appropriate public processes of deliberation which follow the procedures of the Habermasian discourse model. The basic idea behind this model is that:

> only those norms, i.e. general rules of action and institutional arrangements, can be said to be valid which would be agreed to by all those affected by their consequences, if such agreement were reached as a consequence of a process of deliberation which has the following features:
>
> (a) participation in such deliberation is governed by the norms of equality and symmetry; all have the same chance to initiate speech acts, to question, interrogate, and to open debate;
> (b) all have the right to question the assigned topics of conversation;
> (c) all have the right to initiate reflexive arguments about the very rules of the discourse procedure and the way in which they are applied or carried out. There is no *prima facie* rule limiting the agenda or the conversation, nor the identity of the participants, as long as each excluded person or group can justifiably show that they are relevantly affected by the proposed norm under question.[16]

Let us examine this model of deliberative democracy closely. In their attempt to ground legitimacy on *rationality*, these theorists have to distinguish between mere agreement and rational consensus. That is why they assert that the process of public discussion must realize the conditions of ideal discourse. This sets the values of the procedure, which are impartiality and equality, openness and lack of coercion, and unanimity. The combination of those values in the discussion guarantees that its outcome will be legitimate, since it will produce generalizable interests on which all participants can agree.

Habermasians do not deny that there will, of course, be obstacles to the realization of the ideal discourse, but these obstacles are conceived of as *empirical*. They are due to the fact that it is unlikely, given the practical and empirical limitations of social life, that we will ever be completely able to leave all our particular interests aside in order to coincide with our universal rational self. This is why the ideal speech situation is presented as a regulative idea.

However, if we accept Schmitt's insight about the relations of inclusion–exclusion which are necessarily inscribed in the political constitution of 'the people' – which is required by the exercise of democracy – we have to acknowledge that the obstacles to the realization of the ideal speech situation – and to the consensus without exclusion that it would bring about – are inscribed in the democratic logic itself. Indeed, the free and unconstrained public deliberation of all on matters of common concern goes against the democratic requisite of drawing a frontier between 'us' and 'them'. We could say – this time using Derridean terminology – that the very conditions of possibility of the exercise of democracy constitute simultaneously the conditions of impossibility of democratic legitimacy as envisaged by deliberative democracy. Consensus in a liberal-democratic society is – and will always be – the expression of a hegemony and the crystallization of power relations. The frontier that it establishes between what is and what is not legitimate is a political one, and for that reason it should remain contestable. To deny the existence of such a moment of closure, or to present the frontier as dictated by rationality or morality, is to naturalize what should be perceived as a contingent and temporary hegemonic articulation of 'the people' through a particular regime of inclusion–exclusion. The result of such an operation is to reify the identity of the people by reducing it to one of its many possible forms of identification.

PLURALISM AND ITS LIMITS

Because it postulates the availability of a consensus without exclusion, the model of deliberative democracy is unable to envisage liberal-democratic pluralism in an adequate way. Indeed, one could indicate how, in both Rawls and Habermas – to take the best-known representatives of that trend – the very condition for the creation of consensus is the elimination of pluralism from the public sphere.[17] Hence the incapacity of deliberative democracy to provide a convincing refutation of Schmitt's critique of liberal pluralism. It is this critique that I will now examine, to see how it could be answered.

Schmitt's best-known thesis is certainly that the criterion of the political is the friend–enemy distinction. Indeed, for him, the political 'can be understood only in the context of the ever present possibility of the friend-and-enemy grouping'.[18] Because of the way this thesis is generally interpreted, he is often taken to task for neglecting the 'friend' side of his friend–enemy opposition. In his remarks on homogeneity, however, we can find many indications of how this grouping should be envisaged, and this has important implications for his critique of pluralism.

Let us return to the idea that democracy requires political equality, which stems from partaking in a common substance – this, as we have seen, is what Schmitt means by the need for homogeneity. So far, I have stressed the necessity of drawing a frontier between the 'us' and the 'them'. But we can also examine this question by focusing on the 'us' and the nature of the bond that unites its components. Clearly, to assert that the condition of possibility of an 'us' is the existence of a 'them' does not exhaust the subject. Different forms of unity can be established among the components of the 'us'. To be sure, this is not what Schmitt believes, since in his view unity can exist only on the mode of identity. But this is precisely where the problem with his conception lies. It is useful, therefore, to examine both the strengths and the weaknesses of his argument.

By asserting the need for homogeneity in a democracy, Schmitt is telling us something about the kind of bond that is needed if a democratic political community is to exist. In other words, he is analysing the nature of the 'friendship' which defines the 'us' in a democracy. This, for him, is, of course, a way of taking issue with liberalism for not recognizing the need for such a form of commonality, and for advocating pluralism. If we take his target to be the liberal model of interest-group pluralism which postulates that agreement on mere procedures can assure the cohesion of a liberal society, he is no doubt right. Such a vision of a pluralist society is certainly inadequate. Liberalism simply transposes into the public realm the diversity of interests already existing in society and reduces the political moment to the process of negotiation among interests independently of their political expression. There is no place in such a model for a common identity of democratic citizens; citizenship is reduced to a legal status, and the moment of the political constitution of the people is foreclosed. Schmitt's critique of that type of liberalism is convincing, and it is interesting to note that it chimes with what Rawls says when he rejects the 'modus vivendi' model of constitutional democracy because it is very unstable, always liable to dissolution, and declares that the unity it creates is insufficient.

Having discarded the view that grounds it in a mere convergence of interests and a neutral set of procedures, how, then, should we envisage the unity of a pluralist society? Isn't any other type of unity incompatible with the pluralism advocated by liberal societies? On this issue, Schmitt's answer is, of course, unequivocal: there is no place for pluralism inside a democratic political community. Democracy requires the existence of a homogeneous demos, and this precludes any possibility of pluralism. This is why, in his view, there is an insurmountable contradiction between liberal pluralism and democracy. For him, the only possible and legitimate pluralism is a pluralism of states. Rejecting the liberal idea of a world state, he affirms that the political world is a 'pluriverse', not a 'universe'. In his view: 'The political entity cannot by its very nature be universal in the sense of embracing all of humanity and the entire world.'[19]

In *The Concept of the Political* – taking as his target the kind of pluralism advocated by the pluralist school of Harold Laski and G. D. H. Cole – Schmitt argues that the state cannot be considered as one more association among others, which would be on the same level as a church or a trade union. Against liberal theory, whose aim is to transform the state into a voluntary association through the theory of the social contract, he urges us to acknowledge that the political entity is something different and more decisive. For him, to deny this is to deny the political: 'Only as long as the essence of the political is not comprehended or not taken into consideration is it possible to place a political association pluralistically on the same level with religious, cultural, economic, or other associations and permit it to compete with these.'[20]

A few years later, in his important article 'Ethic of State and Pluralistic State', again discussing Laski and Cole, he notes that the actuality of their pluralist theory comes from the fact that it corresponds to the empirical conditions existing in most industrial societies. The current situation is one in which 'the state, in fact, does appear to be largely dependent on social groups, sometimes as sacrifice to, sometimes as result of, their negotiations – an object of compromise among the powerful social and economic groups, an agglomeration of heterogeneous factors, political parties, combines, unions, churches, and so on . . . '.[21] The state is therefore weakened, and becomes some kind of clearing house, a referee between competing factions. Reduced to a purely instrumental function, it cannot be the object of loyalty; it loses its ethical role and its capacity to represent the political unity of a people. While he deplores such a situation, Schmitt none the less admits that as far as their empirical diagnostic is concerned, the pluralists have a point. In his opinion, the interest of their theory lies in the 'appreciation of the concrete empirical power of social groups, and of the empirical situation as it is determined by the ways in which individuals belong to several of such social groups'.[22]

Schmitt, it must be said, does not always see the existence of parties as being absolutely incompatible with the existence of an ethical state. In the same article, he even seems willing to admit at least the possibility of some form of pluralism that does not negate the unity of the state. But he quickly rejects it, declaring that it will inevitably lead to the type of pluralism that will dissolve political unity:

> If the state then becomes a pluralistic party state, the unity of the state can be maintained only as long as two or more parties agree to recognize common premisses. That unity then rests in particular on the constitution recognized by all parties, which must be respected without qualification as the common foundation. The ethic of state then amounts to a constitutional ethic. Depending on the substantivity, unequivocality and authority of the constitution, a very effective unity can be found there. But it can also be the case that the constitution dwindles into mere rules of the game, its ethic of state into a mere ethic of fair play; and that it finally, in a pluralistic dissolution of the unity of the political whole, gets to the point where the unity is only an agglomeration of changing alliances between heterogeneous groups. The constitutional ethic then dwindles even further, to the point of the ethic of state being reduced in the proposition *pacta sunt servanda*.[23]

SCHMITT'S FALSE DILEMMA

I think Schmitt is right to stress the deficiencies of the kind of pluralism that negates the specificity of the political association, and I concur with his assertion that it is necessary to constitute the people *politically*. But I do not believe that this must commit us to denying the possibility of any form of pluralism within the political association. To be sure, liberal theory has so far been unable to provide a convincing solution to this problem. This does not mean, however, that it is insoluble. In fact, Schmitt presents us with a false dilemma: either there is unity of the people, and this requires expelling every division and antagonism outside the demos – the exterior it needs if it is to establish its unity; or some forms of division inside the demos are considered legitimate, and this will lead inexorably to the kind of pluralism which negates political unity and the very existence of the people. As Jean-François Kervégan points out: 'for Schmitt, either the State imposes its order and its rationality to a civil society characterized by pluralism, competition and disorder, or, as is the case in liberal democracy, social pluralism will empty the political entity of its meaning and bring it back to its *other*, the state of nature'.[24]

What leads Schmitt to formulate such a dilemma is the way he envisages political unity. The unity of the state must, for him, be a concrete unity, already given and therefore stable. This is also true of the way he envisages the identity of the people: it also must exist as a given. Because of that, his distinction between 'us' and 'them' is not really politically constructed; it is merely a recognition of already-existing borders. While he rejects the pluralist conception, Schmitt is nevertheless unable to situate himself on a completely different terrain because he retains a view of political and social identities as empirically given. His position is, in fact, ultimately contradictory. On the one hand, he seems seriously to consider the possibility that pluralism could bring about the dissolution of the unity of the state. If that dissolution is, however, a distinctive *political* possibility, it also entails that the existence of such a unity is itself a contingent fact which requires a political construction. On the other hand, however, the unity is presented as a *factum* whose obviousness could ignore the political conditions of its production. Only as a result of this sleight of hand can the alternative be as inexorable as Schmitt wants it to be.

What Schmitt fears most is the loss of common premises and consequent destruction of the political unity which he sees as inherent in the pluralism that accompanies mass democracy. There is certainly a danger of this happening, and his warning should be taken seriously. But this is not a reason to reject all forms of pluralism. I propose to refuse Schmitt's dilemma, while acknowledging his argument for the need of some form of 'homogeneity' in a democracy. The problem we have to face becomes, then, how to imagine in a different way what Schmitt refers to as 'homogeneity' but that – in order to stress the differences with his conception – I propose to call, rather, 'commonality'; how to envisage a form of commonality strong enough to institute a 'demos' but nevertheless compatible with certain forms of pluralism: religious, moral and cultural pluralism, as well as a pluralism of political parties. This is the challenge that engaging with Schmitt's critique forces us to confront. It is indeed a crucial one, since what is at stake is the very formulation of a pluralistic view of democratic citizenship.

I obviously do not pretend to provide a solution within the confines of this chapter, but I would like to suggest some lines of reflection. To offer a different – resolutely non-Schmittian – answer to the compatibility of pluralism and liberal democracy requires, in my view, putting into question any idea of 'the people' as already given, with a substantive identity. What we need to do is precisely what Schmitt does not do: once we have recognized that the unity of the people is the result of a political construction, we need to explore all the logical possibilities that a political articulation entails. Once the identity of the people – or rather, its multiple possible identities – is envisaged on the mode of a political articulation, it is important to stress that if it is to be a real *political* articulation, not merely the acknowledgement of empirical differences, such an identity of the people must be seen as the *result* of the political process of hegemonic articulation. Democratic politics does not consist in the moment when a fully constituted people exercises its rule. The moment of rule is indissociable from the very struggle about the definition of the people, about the constitution of its identity. Such an identity, however, can never be fully constituted, and it can exist only through multiple and competing forms of *identifications*. Liberal democracy is precisely the recognition of this constitutive gap between the people and its various identifications. Hence the importance of leaving this space of contestation forever open, instead of trying to fill it through the establishment of a supposedly 'rational' consensus.

To conceive liberal-democratic politics in such a way is to acknowledge Schmitt's insight into the distinction between 'us' and 'them', because this struggle over the constitution of the people always takes place within a conflictual field, and implies the existence of competing forces. Indeed, there is no hegemonic articulation without the determination of a frontier, the definition of a 'them'. But in the case of liberal-democratic politics this frontier is an internal one, and the 'them' is not a permanent outsider. We can begin to realize, therefore, why such a regime requires pluralism. Without a plurality of competing forces which attempt to define the common good, and aim at fixing the identity of the community, the political articulation of the demos could not take place. We would be in the field either of the aggregation of interests, or of a process of deliberation which eliminates the moment of decision. That is – as Schmitt pointed out – in the field of economics or of ethics, but not in the field of politics.

Nevertheless, by envisaging unity only under the mode of substantive unity, and denying the possibility of pluralism within the political association, Schmitt was unable to grasp that there was another alternative open to liberals, one that could render the articulation between liberalism and democracy viable. What he could not conceive of, owing to the limits of his problematic, he deemed impossible. Since his objective was to attack liberalism, such a move is not surprising but it certainly indicates the limits of his theoretical reflection.

Despite these shortcomings, Schmitt's questioning of liberalism is a very powerful one. It reveals several weaknesses of liberal democracy, and brings its blind spot to the fore. Those deficiencies cannot be ignored. If we are to elaborate a view of democratic society which is convincing and worthy of allegiance, they have to be addressed. Schmitt is an adversary from whom we can learn, because we can draw on his insights. Turning them against him, we should use them to formulate a better understanding of liberal democracy, one that acknowledges its paradoxical nature. Only by coming to terms with the double movement of inclusion–exclusion that democratic politics entails can we deal with the challenge with which the process of globalization confronts us today.

NOTES

1. John Rawls, *Political Liberalism*, New York, 1996, p. lxi.
2. I would have thought everybody should be able to understand that it is

possible to use Schmitt against Schmitt – to use the insights of his critique of liberalism in order to consolidate liberalism – while recognizing that this was not, of course, his aim. However, it does not seem to be the case, since Bill Scheuermann, in *Between the Norm and the Exception* (Cambridge, MA, 1994, p. 8), criticizes me for presenting Schmitt as a theorist of radical pluralist democracy!

3. David Held, *Democracy and the Global Order*, Cambridge, 1995.

4. Richard Falk, *On Human Governance*, Cambridge, 1995.

5. Carl Schmitt, *The Crisis of Parliamentary Democracy*, trans. Ellen Kennedy, Cambridge, MA, 1985, p. 9.

6. Ibid.

7. Ibid., p. 13.

8. Ibid., p. 9.

9. Ibid.

10. Ibid., p. 11.

11. Ibid., p. 12.

12. I have put forward a similar argument about the tension that exists between the articulation of the liberal logic of difference and the democratic logic of equivalence in my discussion of Schmitt in *The Return of the Political*, London, 1993, Chapters 7 and 8.

13. Carl Schmitt, *The Concept of the Political*, trans. George Schwab, New Brunswick, 1976, p. 70.

14. For a critique of the Rawlsian model and its incapacity to acknowledge the *political* nature of the discrimination it establishes between 'simple' and 'reasonable' pluralism, see Chapter 1 in this volume.

15. Seyla Benhabib, 'Deliberative Rationality and Models of Democratic Legitimacy', *Constellations*, 1, 1, April 1994, p. 30.

16. Ibid., p. 31.

17. This, of course, takes place in a different way in both authors. Rawls relegates pluralism to the private sphere, while Habermas screens it out, so to speak, from the public sphere through the procedures of argumentation. In both cases, however, the result is the elimination of pluralism from the public sphere.

18. Schmitt, *The Concept of the Political*, p. 35.

19. Ibid., p. 53.

20. Ibid., p. 45.

21. Carl Schmitt, 'Staatsethik und pluralistischer Staat', *Kantstudien* 35, 1, 1930, translated in Chantal Mouffe (ed.), *The Challenge of Carl Schmitt*, London, 1999, pp. 195–208.

22. Ibid., pp. 195–208.

23. Ibid.

24. Jean-François Kervégan, *Carl Schmitt et Hegel. Le politique entre métaphysique et positivité*, Paris, 1992, p. 259.

3

WITTGENSTEIN, POLITICAL THEORY AND DEMOCRACY

Democratic societies are today confronted with new challenges that they are ill-prepared to answer because they are unable to grasp the nature of the political and to come to terms with the paradox which is at the core of modern liberal democracy. One of the main reasons for this incapacity resides, in my view, in the rationalistic framework which informs the main currents of political theory. It is high time, if we want to be in a condition to consolidate and deepen democratic institutions, to relinquish that framework and to begin thinking about politics in a different way

My argument in this chapter will be that Wittgenstein can help us to carry out such a project. Indeed I consider that we find in his later work many insights that can serve, not only to reveal the limitations of the rationalistic framework, but also to overcome them. With this aim in mind, I will examine a series of central issues in political theory in order to show how a Wittgensteinian perspective could provide an alternative to the rationalist approach. However, I want to indicate at the outset that my intention is neither to extract a political theory from Wittgenstein, nor to attempt elaborating one on the basis of his writings. I believe that Wittgenstein's importance consists in pointing to a *new way of theorizing* about the political, one that breaks with the universalizing and homogenizing mode that has informed most of liberal theory since Hobbes. This is what is urgently needed, not a new system, but a profound shift in the way we approach political questions.

In enquiring about the specificity of this Wittgensteinian new style of theorizing, I will follow the pioneering work of Hanna Pitkin who, in her book *Wittgenstein and Justice*, argues very convincingly that, with his stress on the particular case, on the need to accept plurality and contradiction and the emphasis on the investigating and speaking self, Wittgenstein is particularly helpful for thinking about democracy. According to her, Wittgenstein, like Marx, Nietzsche and Freud, is a key figure to understanding our modern predicament. By examining the craving for certainty, his later philosophy is, she says, 'an attempt to accept and live with the illusionless human condition – relativity, doubt and the absence of God'.[1]

I will also take my bearings from James Tully, who provides one of the most interesting examples of the kind of approach that I am advocating here. For instance, he has used Wittgenstein's insights to criticize a convention widely found in current political thought, the thesis 'that our way of life is free and rational only if it is founded on some form or other of critical reflection'.[2] Examining Jürgen Habermas's picture of critical reflection and justification as well as Charles Taylor's notion of interpretation, and scrutinizing their distinctive grammars, Tully brings to the fore the existence of a multiplicity of languages – games of critical reflection, none of which could pretend to playing the foundational role in our political life. Moreover, in his book *Strange Multiplicity*,[3] he has shown how such an approach can be used not only to criticize the imperial and monological form of reasoning which is constitutive of modern constitutionalism but also to develop what he calls a 'post-imperial' philosophy and practice of constitutionalism.

UNIVERSALISM VERSUS CONTEXTUALISM

Let's begin by scrutinizing the debate between contextualists and universalists. One of the most contentious issues among political theorists in recent years is at the centre of that debate and it is a crucial one, since it concerns the very nature of liberal democracy. Should liberal democracy be envisaged as the rational solution to the political question of how to organize human coexistence? Does it therefore embody the just society, the one that should be universally accepted by all rational and reasonable individuals? Or does it merely represent one form of political order among other possible ones? A political form of human coexistence, which, under certain conditions, can be deemed 'just', but that must also be seen as the product of a particular history, with specific historical, cultural and geographical conditions of existence.

This is indeed a crucial question because, if this second view is the correct one, we have to acknowledge that there might be other just political forms of society, products of other contexts. Liberal democracy should therefore renounce its claim to universality. It is worth stressing that those who argue along those lines insist that, contrary to what the universalists declare, such a position does not necessarily entail accepting a relativism that would justify *any* political system. What it requires is envisaging a *plurality* of legitimate answers to the question of what is the just political order. However, political judgement would not be made irrelevant, since it would still be possible to discriminate between just and unjust regimes.

It is clear that what is at stake in this debate is the very nature of political theory. Two different positions confront each other. On one side we find the 'rationalist-universalists' who – like Ronald Dworkin, the early Rawls and Habermas – assert that the aim of political theory is to establish universal truths, valid for all independently of the historico-cultural context. Of course, for them, there can only be one answer to the enquiry about the 'good regime', and many of their efforts consist in proving that constitutional democracy is the regime that fulfils those requirements.

It is in intimate connection with this debate that one should tackle another disputed question, which concerns the elaboration of a theory of justice. It is only when located in this wider context that one can really grasp, for instance, the implications of the view put forward by a universalist like Dworkin when he declares that a theory of justice must call on general principles and its objective must be to 'try to find some inclusive formula that can be used to measure social justice in any society'.[4]

The universalist-rationalist approach is currently the dominant one in political theory, but it is being challenged by another one that can be called 'contextualist' and which is of particular interest for us because it is clearly influenced by Wittgenstein. Contextualists like Michael Walzer and Richard Rorty deny the availability of a point of view that could be situated outside the practices and the institutions of a given culture and from where universal, 'context-independent' judgements could be made. This is why Walzer argues against the idea that the political theorist should try to adopt a position detached from all forms of particular allegiances in order to judge impartially and objectively. In his view, the theorist should 'stay in the cave' and assume fully his or her status as a member of a particular community; and this role consists in interpreting for fellow citizens the world of meanings that they have in common.[5]

Using several Wittgensteinian insights, the contextualist approach problematizes the kind of liberal reasoning that envisages the common framework for argumentation on the model of a 'neutral' or 'rational' dialogue. Indeed, Wittgenstein's views lead to undermining the very basis of this form of reasoning since, as it has been pointed out, he reveals that:

> Whatever there is of definite content in contractarian deliberation and its deliverance, derives from particular judgments we are inclined to make as practitioners of specific forms of life. The forms of life in which we find ourselves are themselves held together by a network of precontractual agreements, without which there would be no possibility of mutual understanding or therefore, of disagreement.[6]

According to the contextualist approach, liberal-democratic institutions must be seen as defining one possible political 'language-game' among others. Since they do not provide the rational solution to the problem of human coexistence, it is futile to search for arguments in their favour which would not be 'context-dependent' in order to secure them against other political language-games. By envisaging the issue according to a Wittgensteinian perspective, such an approach brings to the fore the inadequacy of all attempts to give a rational foundation to liberal-democratic principles by arguing that they would be chosen by rational individuals in idealized conditions like the 'veil of ignorance' (Rawls) or the 'ideal speech situation' (Habermas). As Peter Winch has indicated with respect to Rawls, 'The "veil of ignorance" that characterizes his position runs foul of Wittgenstein's point that what is "reasonable" cannot be characterized independently of the *content* of certain pivotal "judgments".'[7]

For his part, Richard Rorty – who proposes a 'neo-pragmatic' reading of Wittgenstein – has affirmed, taking issue with Apel and Habermas, that it is not possible to derive a universalistic moral philosophy from the philosophy of language. There is nothing, for him, in the nature of language that could serve as a basis for justifying to all possible audiences the superiority of liberal democracy. He declares: 'We should have to abandon the hopeless task of finding politically neutral premises, premises which can be justified to anybody, from which to infer an obligation to pursue democratic politics.'[8] He considers that envisaging democratic advances as if they were linked to progress in rationality is not helpful, and that we should stop presenting the institutions of liberal western societies as the solution that other people will necessarily adopt when they cease to be 'irrational' and become 'modern'. Following Wittgenstein, he sees the question at stake as one not of rationality but of shared beliefs. To call somebody irrational in this context, he states, 'is not to say that she is not making proper use of her mental faculties. It is only to say that she does not seem to share enough beliefs and desires with one to make conversation with her on the disputed point fruitful.'[9]

Approaching democratic action from a Wittgensteinian point of view can therefore help us to pose the question of allegiance to democracy in a different way. Indeed, we are led to acknowledge that democracy does not require a theory of truth and notions like unconditionality and universal validity but a manifold of practices and pragmatic moves aiming at persuading people to broaden the range of their commitments to others, to build a more inclusive community. Such a shift in perspective reveals that, by putting an exclusive emphasis on the arguments needed to secure the *legitimacy* of liberal institutions, recent moral and political theorists have been asking the wrong question. The real issue is not to find arguments to justify the rationality or universality of liberal democracy that would be acceptable by every rational or reasonable person. Liberal democratic principles can only be defended as being constitutive of our form of life, and we should not try to ground our commitment to them on something supposedly safer. As Richard Flathman – another political theorist influenced by Wittgenstein – indicates, the agreements that exist on many features of liberal democracy do not need to be supported by certainty in any of the philosophical senses. In his view, 'Our agreements in these judgements consti-tute the language of our politics. It is a language arrived at and continuously modified through no less than a history of dis-course, a history in which we have thought about, as we became able to think in, that language.'[10]

Rorty's appropriation of Wittgenstein is very useful for criticiz-ing the pretensions of Kantian-inspired philosophers like Haber-mas who want to find a viewpoint standing above politics from which one could guarantee the superiority of liberal democracy. But I think that Rorty departs from Wittgenstein when he envisages moral and political progress in terms of the universaliz-ation of the liberal-democratic model. Oddly enough, on this point he comes very close to Habermas. To be sure, there is an important difference between them. Habermas believes that such a process of universalization will take place through rational argumentation and that it requires arguments from transculturally valid premises to justify the superiority of western liberalism. Rorty, for his part, sees it as a matter of persuasion and economic progress, and he imagines that it depends on people having more secure conditions of existence and sharing more beliefs and desires with others. Hence his conviction that through economic growth and the right kind of 'sentimental education' a universal consensus could be built around liberal institutions. What he never puts into question, however, is the very belief in the superiority of the liberal way of life, and on that count he is not faithful to his Wittgensteinian inspiration. One could indeed make to him the reproach that Wittgenstein made to James George Frazer in his 'Remarks on Frazer's *Golden Bough*' when he commented that it seemed impossible for Frazer to understand a different way of life from the one of his time.

DEMOCRACY AS SUBSTANCE OR AS PROCEDURES

There is a second domain in political theory in which an approach inspired by Wittgenstein's conception of practices and language-games could also contribute to elaborate an alternative to the rationalistic framework. It is constituted by the set of issues related to the nature of procedures and their role in the modern conception of democracy.

The crucial idea provided by Wittgenstein in this field is when he asserts that to have agreements in opinions, there must first be agreement on the language used. And the fact that he stresses that those agreements in opinions are agreements in forms of life. As he says:

So you are saying that human agreement decides what is true and what is false. It is what human beings *say* that is true and false; and they agree in the *language* they use. That is not agreement in opinions but in forms of life.[11]

With respect to the question of 'procedures', which is the one that I want to highlight here, this points to the necessity for a considerable number of 'agreements in judgements' to already exist in a society before a given set of procedures can work. Indeed, according to Wittgenstein, to agree on the definition of a term is not enough, and we need agreement in the way we use it. He puts it in the following way: 'if language is to be a means of communication there must be agreement not only in definitions but also (queer as this may sound) in judgements'.[12]

This reveals that procedures only exist as complex ensembles of practices. Those practices constitute specific forms of individuality and identity that make possible the allegiance to the procedures. It is because they are inscribed in shared forms of life and agreements in judgements that procedures can be accepted and followed. They cannot be seen as rules that are created on the basis of principles and then applied to specific cases. Rules, for Wittgenstein, are always abridgements of practices, they are inseparable from specific forms of life. The distinction between procedural and substantial cannot therefore be as clear as most liberal theorists would have it. In the case of justice, for instance, it means that one cannot oppose, as so many liberals do, procedural and substantial justice without recognizing that procedural justice already presupposes acceptance of certain values. It is the *liberal* conception of justice which posits the priority of the right over the good, but this is already the expression of a specific good. Democracy is not only a matter of establishing the right procedures independently of the practices that make possible democratic forms of individuality. The question of the conditions of existence of democratic forms of individuality and of the practices and language-games in which they are constituted is a central one, even in a liberal-democratic society where procedures play a central role. Procedures always involve substantial ethical commitments. For that reason they cannot work properly if they are not supported by a specific form of ethos.

This last point is very important, since it forces us to acknowledge something that the dominant liberal model is unable to recognize, namely, that a liberal-democratic conception of justice and liberal-democratic institutions require a democratic ethos in order to function properly and maintain themselves. This is, for instance, precisely what Habermas's discourse theory of procedural democracy is unable to grasp because of the sharp distinction that Habermas wants to draw between moral-practical discourses and ethical-practical discourses. It is not enough to state as he now does, criticizing Apel, that a discourse theory of democracy cannot be based only on the formal pragmatic conditions of communication and that it must take account of legal, moral, ethical and pragmatic argumentation.

DEMOCRATIC CONSENSUS AND AGONISTIC PLURALISM

My argument is that, by providing a practice-based account of rationality, Wittgenstein in his later work opens a much more promising way for thinking about political questions and for envisaging the task of a democratic politics than the rationalist-universalist framework. In the present conjuncture, characterized by an increasing disaffection towards democracy – despite its apparent triumph – it is vital to understand how a strong adhesion to democratic values and institutions can be established and why rationalism constitutes an obstacle to such an understanding. It is necessary to realize that it is not by offering sophisticated rational arguments and by making context-transcendent truth claims about the superiority of liberal democracy that democratic values can be fostered. The creation of democratic forms of individuality is a question of *identification* with democratic values, and this is a complex process that takes place through a manifold of practices, discourses and language-games.

A Wittgensteinian approach in political theory could play an important role in the fostering of democratic values because it allows us to grasp the conditions of emergence of a democratic consensus. As Wittgenstein says:

> Giving grounds, however, justifying the evidence, comes to an end – but the end is not certain propositions striking us immediately as true, i.e. it is not a kind of *seeing* on our part; it is our *acting*, which lies at the bottom of the language-game.[13]

For him, agreement is established not on significations (*Meinungen*) but on forms of life (*Lebensform*). It is *Einstimmung*, fusion of voices made possible by a common form of life, not *Einverstand*, product of reason – like in Habermas. This, I believe, is of crucial importance and it not only indicates the nature of every consensus but also reveals its limits:

> Where two principles really do meet which cannot be reconciled with one another, then each man declares the other a fool and an heretic. I said I would 'combat' the other man, – but wouldn't I give him reasons? Certainly; but how far do they go? At the end of reasons comes *persuasion*.[14]

I take this emphasis on the limits of giving reasons to constitute an important starting point for elaborating an alternative to the current model of 'deliberative democracy' with its rationalistic conception of communication and its misguided search for a consensus that would be fully inclusive. Indeed, I see the 'agonistic pluralism' that I have been advocating[15] as inspired by a Wittgensteinian mode of theorizing and as attempting to develop what I take to be one of his fundamental insights: grasping what it means to follow a rule.

At this point in my argumentation, it is useful to bring in the reading of Wittgenstein proposed by James Tully because it chimes with my approach. Tully is interested in showing how Wittgenstein's philosophy represents an alternative worldview to the one that informs modern constitutionalism, so his concerns are not exactly the same as mine. But there are several points of contact and many of his reflections are directly relevant for my purpose. Of particular importance is the way he examines how in the *Philosophical Investigations*, Wittgenstein envisages the correct way to understand general terms. According to Tully, we can find two lines of argument. The first consists in showing that 'understanding a general term is not a theoretical activity of interpreting and applying a general theory or rule in particular cases'.[16] Wittgenstein indicates, using examples of signposts and maps, how I can always be in doubt about the way I should interpret the rule and follow it. He says, for instance:

A rule stands there like a sign-post. – Does it shew which direction I am to take when I have passed it; whether along the road or the footpath or cross-country? But where is it said which way I am to follow it; whether in the direction of its finger or (e.g.) in the opposite one?[17]

As a consequence, notes Tully, a general rule cannot 'account for precisely the phenomenon we associate with understanding the meaning of a general term: the ability to use a general term, as well as to question its accepted use, in various circumstances without recursive doubts'.[18] This should lead us to abandon the idea that the rule and its interpretation 'determine meaning' and to recognize that understanding a general term does not consist in grasping a theory but coincides with the ability of using it in different circumstances. For Wittgenstein, 'obeying a rule' is a practice and our understanding of rules consists in the mastery of a technique. The use of general terms is therefore to be seen as intersubjective 'practices' or 'customs' not that different from games like chess or tennis. This is why Wittgenstein insists that it is a mistake to envisage every action according to a rule as an 'interpretation' and that 'there is a way of grasping a rule which is *not* an *interpretation*, but which is exhibited in what we call "obeying the rule" and "going against it" in actual cases'.[19]

Tully considers that the wide-ranging consequences of this point are missed when one affirms, like Peter Winch, that people using general terms in daily activities are still following rules but that those rules are implicit or background understandings shared by all members of a culture. He argues that this is to retain the view of communities as homogeneous wholes and to neglect Wittgenstein's second argument, which consists in showing that 'the multiplicity of uses is too various, tangled, contested and creative to be governed by rules'.[20] For Wittgenstein, instead of trying to reduce all games to what they *must* have in common, we should 'look and see whether there is something that is common to all' and what we will see is 'similarities, relationships, and a whole series of them' whose result constitutes 'a complicated network of similarities overlapping and criss-crossing', similarities that he characterizes as 'family resemblances'.[21]

I submit that this is a crucial insight which undermines the very objective that those who advocate the 'deliberative' approach present as the aim of democracy: the establishment of a rational consensus on universal principles. They believe that through rational deliberation an impartial standpoint could be reached where decisions would be taken that are equally in the interests of all.[22] Wittgenstein, on the contrary, suggests another view. If we follow his lead, we should acknowledge and valorize the diversity of ways in which the 'democratic game' can be played, instead of trying to reduce this diversity to a uniform model of citizenship. This would mean fostering a plurality of forms of being a democratic citizen and creating the institutions that would make it possible to follow the democratic rules in a plurality of ways. What Wittgenstein teaches us is that there cannot be one single best, more 'rational' way to obey those rules and that it is precisely such a recognition that is constitutive of a pluralist democracy. 'Following a rule', says Wittgenstein, 'is analogous to obeying an order. We are trained to do so; we react to an order in a particular way. But what if one person reacts in one way and another in another to the order and the training? Which one is right?'[23] This is indeed a crucial question for democratic theory. And it cannot be resolved, pace the rationalists, by claiming that there is a correct understanding of the rule that every rational person should accept. To be sure, we need to be able to distinguish between 'obeying the rule' and 'going against it'. But space needs to be provided for the many different practices in which obedience to the democratic rules can be inscribed. And this should not be envisaged as a temporary accommodation, as a stage in the process leading to the realization of the rational consensus, but as a constitutive feature of a democratic society. Democratic citizenship can take many diverse forms and such a diversity, far from being a danger for democracy, is in fact its very condition of existence. This will, of course, create conflict and it would be a mistake to expect all those different understandings to coexist without clashing. But this struggle will not be one between 'enemies' but among 'adversaries', since all participants will recognize the positions of the others in the contest as legitimate ones. Such an understanding of democratic politics, which is precisely what I call 'agonistic pluralism', is unthinkable within a rationalistic problematic which, by necessity, tends to erase diversity. A perspective inspired by Wittgenstein, on the contrary, can contribute to its formulation, and this is why his contribution to democratic thinking is invaluable.

WITTGENSTEIN AND RESPONSIBILITY

I would like to end, however, by raising a word of caution. Several roads can be followed by those who share a Wittgensteinian understanding of the centrality of practices and forms of life, and they do not all have the same consequences for thinking about democracy. Indeed, even among those who agree on the significance of Wittgenstein's later work, there are significant divergences which have implications for the new way of political theorizing that I am advocating.

I consider, for instance, that the criticisms levelled by Stanley Cavell against the assimilation between Wittgenstein and Pragmatism raise important questions with respect to the nature of the democratic project. For Cavell, when Wittgenstein says: 'If I have exhausted the justifications I have reached bedrock, and my spade is turned. Then I am inclined to say: "This is simply what I do",'[24] he is not making a typically pragmatic move and defending a view of language according to which certainty between words and world would be based on action. In Cavell's view, 'this is an expression less of action than of passion, or of impotency expressed as potency'.[25] Discussing Kripke's reading of Wittgenstein as making a sceptical discovery to which he gives a sceptical solution, Cavell also argues that this misses the fact that for Wittgenstein:

> skepticism is neither true nor false but a standing human threat to the human; that this absence of the victor helps articulate the fact that, in a democracy embodying good enough justice, the conversation over how good its justice is must take place and must also not have a victor, that this is not because agreement can or should always be reached but because disagreement, and separateness of position, is to be allowed its satisfactions, reached and expressed in particular ways.[26]

This has far-reaching implications for politics, since it precludes the type of self-complacent understanding of liberal democracy for which, for instance, many have criticized pragmatists like Richard Rorty. A radical reading of Wittgenstein needs to emphasize – in the way Cavell does in his critique of Rawls[27] – that bringing a conversation to a close is always a personal choice, a *decision* which cannot be simply presented as mere application of procedures and justified as the only move that we could make in those circumstances.

Using Wittgensteinian insights, Cavell has indeed pointed out that Rawls's account of justice omits a very important dimension of what takes place when we assess the claims made upon us in the name of justice in situations in which it is the degree of society's compliance with its ideal that is in question. He has taken issue with Rawls's assertion that 'Those who express resentment must be prepared to show why certain institutions are unjust or how others have injured them.'[28] In Rawls's view, if they are unable to do so, we can consider that our conduct is above reproach and bring the conversation to a close. But, asks Cavell, 'what if there is a cry of justice that expresses a sense not of having lost out in an unequal yet fair struggle, but of having from the start been left out'.[29] Giving as example the situation of Nora in Ibsen's play *A Doll's House*, he shows how deprivation of a voice in the conversation of justice can be the work of the moral consensus itself. He argues, faithful in that to his Wittgensteinian inspiration, that we should never refuse bearing responsibility for our decisions by invoking the commands of general rules or principles.

I consider that Cavell is right to stress that what Wittgenstein's philosophy exemplifies is not a quest for certainty but a quest for responsibility, and that what he teaches us is that entering a claim is making an assertion and is something that humans *do* and for which they should be responsible. This emphasis on the moment of *decision* and on *responsibility* enables us to envisage democratic politics in a different way because it subverts the ever-present temptation in democratic societies to disguise existing forms of exclusion under the veil of rationality or of morality. By precluding the possibility of a complete reabsorption of alterity into 'oneness and harmony', this insistence on the need to leave the conversation on justice for ever open establishes the basis for a project of 'radical and plural democracy'.[30]

It is worth stressing that a reading like Cavell's brings to light many important points of convergence between Wittgenstein and Derrida's account of undecidability and ethical responsibility.[31] In the perspective of deconstruction,

> The undecidable remains caught, lodged, at least as a ghost – but an essential ghost – in every decision, in every event of decision. Its ghostliness deconstructs from within any assurance of presence, any certitude or any supposed criteriology that would assure us of the justice of a decision.[32]

For Derrida, as for Wittgenstein, understanding responsibility requires that we give up the dream of total mastery and the fantasy that we could escape from our human forms of life. Both of them provide us with a new way of thinking about democracy that departs fundamentally from the dominant-rationalist approach. A democratic thinking that incorporates their insights can be more receptive to the multiplicity of voices that a pluralist society encompasses and to the need to allow them forms of expression instead of striving towards harmony and consensus. Indeed it acknowledges that, in order to impede the closure of the democratic space, it is necessary to abandon any reference to the idea of a consensus that, because it would be grounded on justice and rationality, could not be destabilized. The main obstacle to such a 'radical-pluralistic-democratic' vision is constituted by the misguided quest for consensus and reconciliation, and this is something that Wittgenstein, with his insistence on the need to respect differences, brings to the fore in a very powerful way.

NOTES

1. Hanna Pitkin, *Wittgenstein and Justice*, Berkeley, 1972, p. 337.

2. James Tully, 'Wittgenstein and Political Philosophy', *Political Theory* 17, 2, May 1989, p. 172.

3. James Tully, *Strange Multiplicity: Constitutionalism in an Age of Diversity*, Cambridge, 1995.

4. Ronald Dworkin, *New York Review of Books*, 17 April 1983.

5. Michael Walzer, *Spheres of Justice*, New York, 1983, p.xiv.

6. John Gray, *Liberalisms: Essays in Political Philosophy*, London and New York, 1989, p. 252.

7. Peter Winch, 'Certainty and Authority', in A. Philipps Griffiths (ed.), *Wittgenstein Centenary Essays*, Cambridge, 1991, p. 235.

8. Richard Rorty, 'Sind Aussagen universelle Geltungsanspruche?', *Deutsche Zeitschrift für Philosophie*, 6, 1994, p. 986.

9. Richard Rorty, 'Justice as a Larger Loyalty', paper presented at the Seventh East–West Philosophers Conference, University of Hawaii, January 1995, published in *Justice and Democracy: Cross-Cultural Perspectives*, ed. R. Botenkoe and M. Stepaniants, University of Hawaii Press, 1997, p. 19.

10. Richard E. Flathman, *Towards a Liberalism*, Ithaca and London, 1989, p. 63.

11. Ludwig Wittgenstein, *Philosophical Investigations*, I, 241, Oxford, 1953.

12. Ibid., I, 242.

13. Ludwig Wittgenstein, *On Certainty*, London, 1969, p. 204.

14. Ibid., pp. 611–12.

15. See in that respect Chantal Mouffe, *The Return of the Political*, London, 1993.

16. Tully, *Strange Multiplicity*, p. 105.

17. Wittgenstein, *Philosophical Investigations*, I, 85.

18. Ibid.

19. Ibid., 201.

20. Tully, *Strange Multiplicity*, p. 107.

21. Wittgenstein, *Philosophical Investigations*, I, 66 and 67.

22. There are many versions of the 'deliberative democracy' model, some more rationalistic than others. But they all share the view that the western form of democracy is the superior one and that its institutions have a culture-transcending validity due to their higher level of rationality. For a modified Habermasian version of that model, see Seyla Benhabib, 'Deliberative

Rationality and Models of Democratic Legitimacy', *Constellations* 1, 1, April 1994.

23. Wittgenstein, *Philosophical Investigations*, I, 206.

24. Ibid., 217.

25. Stanley Cavell, *Conditions Handsome and Unhandsome*, Chicago, 1988, p. 21.

26. Ibid., p. 24.

27. For this criticism of Rawls by Cavell see Chapter 3 of his *Conditions Handsome and Unhandsome*.

28. John Rawls, *A Theory of Justice*, Cambridge, MA, 1971, p. 533.

29. Cavell, *Conditions Handsome and Unhandsome*, p. xxxviii.

30. This vision of 'radical and plural democracy' is elaborated in Ernesto Laclau and Chantal Mouffe, *Hegemony and Socialist Strategy: Towards a Radical Democratic Politics*, London, 1985.

31. The existence of several points of convergence between Wittgenstein and Derrida is also argued, from a different point of view, in the very interesting book by Henry Staten, *Wittgenstein and Derrida*, Oxford, 1985.

32. Jacques Derrida, 'Force of Law: The "Mystical Foundation of Authority"', in D. Cornell et al. (eds), *Deconstruction and the Possibility of Justice*, New York, 1992, p. 24.

4

FOR AN AGONISTIC MODEL OF DEMOCRACY

As this turbulent century draws to a close, liberal democracy seems to be recognized as the only legitimate form of government. But does that indicate its final victory over its adversaries, as some would have it? There are serious reasons to be sceptical about such a claim. For once, it is not clear how strong is the present consensus and how long it will last. While very few dare to openly challenge the liberal-democratic model, the signs of disaffection with present institutions are becoming widespread. An increasing number of people feel that traditional parties have ceased to take their interests into account, and extreme right-wing parties are making important inroads in many European countries. Moreover, even among those who are resisting the call of the demagogues, there is a marked cynicism about politics and politicians, and this has a very corrosive effect on popular adhesion to democratic values. There is clearly a negative force at work in most liberal-democratic societies, which contradicts the triumphalism that we have witnessed since the collapse of Soviet communism.

It is with those considerations in mind that I will be examining the present debate in democratic theory. I want to evaluate the proposals that democratic theorists are offering in order to consolidate democratic institutions. I will concentrate my attention on the new paradigm of democracy, the model of 'deliberative democracy', which is currently becoming the fastest-growing trend in the field. To be sure, the main idea – that in a democratic polity political decisions should be reached through a process of deliberation among free and equal citizens – has accompanied democracy since its birth in fifth-century Athens. The ways of envisaging deliberation and the constituency of those entitled to deliberate have varied greatly, but deliberation has long played a central role in democratic thought. What we see today is therefore the revival of an old theme, not the sudden emergence of a new one.

What needs scrutinizing, though, is the reason for this renewed interest in deliberation, as well as its current modalities. One explanation has certainly to do with the problems facing democratic societies today. Indeed, one proclaimed aim of deliberative democrats is to offer an alternative to the understanding of democracy which has become dominant in the second half of the twentieth century, the 'aggregative model'. Such a model was initiated by Joseph Schumpeter's seminal work of 1947, *Capitalism, Socialism and Democracy*,[1] which argued that, with the development of mass democracy, popular sovereignty as understood by the classical model of democracy had become inadequate. A new understanding of democracy was needed, putting the emphasis on aggregation of preferences, taking place through political parties for which people would have the capacity to vote at regular intervals. Hence Schumpeter's proposal to define democracy as the system in which people have the opportunity of accepting or rejecting their leaders thanks to a competitive electoral process.

Further developed by theorists like Anthony Downs in *An*

Economic Theory of Democracy,[2] the aggregative model became the standard one in the field which called itself 'empirical political theory'. The aim of this current was to elaborate a descriptive approach to democracy, in opposition to the classical normative one. The authors who adhered to this school considered that under modern conditions, notions like 'common good' and 'general will' had to be relinquished and that the pluralism of interests and values had to be acknowledged as coextensive with the very idea of 'the people'. Moreover, given that in their view, self-interest was what moved individuals to act, not the moral belief that they should do what was in the interests of the community, they declared that it was interests and preferences that should constitute the lines over which political parties should be organized and provide the matter over which bargaining and voting would take place. Popular participation in the taking of decisions should rather be discouraged, since it could only have dysfunctional consequences for the working of the system. Stability and order were more likely to result from compromise among interests than from mobilizing people towards an illusory consensus on the common good. As a consequence, democratic politics was separated from its normative dimension and began to be envisaged from a purely instrumentalist standpoint.

The dominance of the aggregative view, with its reduction of democracy to procedures for the treatment of interest-group pluralism, is what the new wave of normative political theory, inaugurated by John Rawls in 1971 with the publication of his book *A Theory of Justice*,[3] began to put into question and that the deliberative model is today challenging. They declare it to be at the origin of the current disaffection with democratic institutions and of the rampant crisis of legitimacy affecting western democracies. The future of liberal democracy, in their view, depends on recovering its moral dimension. While not denying 'the fact of pluralism' (Rawls) and the necessity to make room for many different conceptions of the good, deliberative democrats affirm that it is nevertheless possible to reach a consensus that would be deeper than a 'mere agreement on procedures', a consensus that could qualify as 'moral'.

DELIBERATIVE DEMOCRACY: ITS AIMS

In wanting to offer an alternative to the dominant aggregative perspective, with its impoverished view of the democratic process, deliberative democrats are, of course, not alone. The specificity of their approach resides in promoting a form of *normative* rationality. Distinctive is also their attempt to provide a solid basis of allegiance to liberal democracy by reconciling the idea of democratic sovereignty with the defence of liberal institutions. Indeed, it is worth stressing that, while critical of a certain type of modus-vivendi liberalism, most of the advocates of deliberative democracy are not anti-liberals. Unlike previous Marxist critics, they stress the central role of liberal values in the modern conception of democracy. Their aim is not to relinquish liberalism but to recover its moral dimension and establish a close link between liberal values and democracy.

Their central claim is that it is possible, thanks to adequate procedures of deliberation, to reach forms of agreement that would satisfy both rationality (understood as defence of liberal rights) and democratic legitimacy (as represented by popular sovereignty). Their move consists in reformulating the democratic principle of popular sovereignty in such a way as to eliminate the dangers that it could pose to liberal values. It is the consciousness of those dangers that has often made liberals wary of popular participation and keen to find ways to discourage or limit it. Deliberative democrats believe that those perils can be avoided, thereby allowing liberals to embrace the democratic ideals with much more enthusiasm than they have done so far. One proposed solution is to reinterpret popular sovereignty in intersubjective terms and to redefine it as 'communicatively generated power'.[4]

There are many different versions of deliberative democracy but they can roughly be classified under two main schools, the first broadly influenced by John Rawls, and the second by Jürgen Habermas. I will therefore concentrate on these two authors, jointly with two of their followers, Joshua Cohen, for the Rawlsian side, Seyla Benhabib, for the Habermasian one. I am of course not denying that there are differences between the two approaches – which I will indicate during my discussion – but there are also important convergences which, from the point of view of my enquiry, are more significant than the disagreements.

As I have already indicated, one of the aims of the deliberative approach – an aim shared by both Rawls and Habermas – consists in securing a strong link between democracy and liberalism, refuting all those critics who – from the right as well as from the left – have proclaimed the contradictory nature of liberal democracy. Rawls, for instance, declares that his ambition is to elaborate a democratic liberalism which would answer to the claim of both liberty and equality. He wants to find a solution to the disagreement which has existed in democratic thought over the past centuries,

between the tradition associated with Locke, which gives greater weight to what Constant called 'the liberties of the moderns', freedom of thought and conscience, certain basic rights of the person and of property and the rule of law, and the tradition associated with Rousseau, which gives greater weight to what Constant called the 'liberties of the ancients', the equal political liberties and the values of public life.[5]

As far as Habermas is concerned, his recent book *Between Facts and Norms* makes it clear that one of the objectives of his procedural theory of democracy is to bring to the fore the 'co-originality' of fundamental individual rights and of popular sovereignty. On one side self-government serves to protect individual rights; on the other side, those rights provide the necessary conditions for the exercise of popular sovereignty. Once they are envisaged in such a way, he says, 'then one can understand how popular sovereignty and human rights go hand in hand, and hence grasp the co-originality of civic and private autonomy'.[6]

Their followers Cohen and Benhabib also stress the reconciliatory move present in the deliberative project. While Cohen states that it is mistaken to envisage the 'liberties of the moderns' as being exterior to the democratic process and that egalitarian and liberal values are to be seen as elements of democracy rather than as constraints upon it,[7] Benhabib declares that the deliberative model can transcend the dichotomy between the liberal emphasis on individual rights and liberties and the democratic emphasis on collective formation and will-formation.[8]

Another point of convergence between the two versions of deliberative democracy is their common insistence on the possibility of grounding authority and legitimacy on some forms of public reasoning and their shared belief in a form of rationality which is not merely instrumental but has a normative dimension:

the 'reasonable' for Rawls, 'communicative rationality' for Habermas. In both cases a strong separation is established between 'mere agreement' and 'rational consensus', and the proper field of politics is identified with the exchange of arguments among reasonable persons guided by the principle of impartiality.

Both Habermas and Rawls believe that we can find in the institutions of liberal democracy the idealized content of practical rationality. Where they diverge is in their elucidation of the form of practical reason embodied in democratic institutions. Rawls emphasizes the role of principles of justice reached through the device of the 'original position' that forces the participants to leave aside all their particularities and interests. His conception of 'justice as fairness' – which states the priority of basic liberal principles – jointly with the 'constitutional essentials' provides the framework for the exercise of 'free public reason'. As far as Habermas is concerned, he defends what he claims to be a strictly proceduralist approach in which no limits are put on the scope and content of the deliberation. It is the procedural constraints of the ideal speech situation that will eliminate the positions which cannot be agreed to by the participants in the moral 'discourse'. As recalled by Benhabib, the features of such a discourse are the following:

(1) participation in such deliberation is governed by the norms of equality and symmetry; all have the same chances to initiate speech acts, to question, to interrogate, and to open debate; (2) all have the right to question the assigned topics of the conversation; and (3) all have the right to initiate reflexive arguments about the very rules of the discourse procedure and the way in which they are applied and carried out. There are no prima facie rules limiting the agenda of the

conversation, or the identity of the participants, as long as any excluded person or group can justifiably show that they are relevantly affected by the proposed norm under question.[9]

For this perspective the basis of legitimacy of democratic institutions derives from the fact that the instances which claim obligatory power do so on the presumption that their decisions represent an impartial standpoint which is equally in the interests of all. Cohen, after stating that democratic legitimacy arises from collective decisions among equal members, declares: 'According to a *deliberative* conception, a decision is collective just in case it emerges from arrangements of binding collective choices that establish conditions of *free public reasoning among equals who are governed by the decisions.*'[10]

In such a view it is not enough for a democratic procedure to take account of the interests of all and to reach a compromise that will establish a modus vivendi. The aim is to generate 'communicative power' and this requires establishing the conditions for a freely given assent of all concerned, hence the importance of finding procedures that would guarantee moral impartiality. Only then can one be sure that the consensus that is obtained is a rational one and not a mere agreement. This is why the accent is put on the nature of the deliberative procedure and on the types of reasons that are deemed acceptable for competent participants. Benhabib puts it in the following way:

According to the deliberative model of democracy, it is a necessary condition for attaining legitimacy and rationality with regard to collective decision making processes in a polity, that the institutions of this polity are so arranged that what is considered in the common interest of all results from processes of collective deliberation conducted rationally and fairly among free and equal individuals.[11]

For the Habermasians, the process of deliberation is guaranteed to have reasonable outcomes to the extent that it realizes the condition of the 'ideal discourse': the more equal and impartial, the more open the process is, and the less the participants are coerced and ready to be guided by the force of the better argument, the more likely truly generalizable interests will be accepted by all those relevantly affected. Habermas and his followers do not deny that there will be obstacles to the realization of the ideal discourse, but those obstacles are conceived as *empirical* ones. They are due to the fact that it is unlikely, given the practical and empirical limitations of social life, that we will ever be able to completely leave aside all our particular interests in order to coincide with our universal rational self. This is why the ideal speech situation is presented as a 'regulative idea'.

Moreover, Habermas now accepts that there are issues that have to remain outside the practices of rational public debate, like existential issues which concern not questions of 'justice' but the 'good life' – this is for him the domain of ethics – or conflicts between interest groups about distributive problems that can only be resolved by means of compromises. But he considers that 'this differentiation within the field of issues that requires political decisions negates neither the prime importance of moral considerations nor the practicability of rational debate as the very form of political communication'.[12] In his view fundamental political questions belong to the same category as moral questions and they can be decided rationally. Contrary to ethical questions, they do not depend on their context. The validity of their answers comes from an independent source and has a universal reach. He remains adamant that the exchange of arguments and counter-arguments as envisaged by his approach is the most suitable procedure for reaching the rational formation of the will from which the general interest will emerge.

Deliberative democracy, in both versions considered here, does concede to the aggregative model that under modern conditions a plurality of values and interests must be acknowledged and that consensus on what Rawls calls 'comprehensive' views of a religious, moral or philosophical nature has to be relinquished. But its advocates do not accept that this entails the impossibility of a rational consensus on political decisions, understanding by that not a simple modus vivendi but a moral type of agreement resulting from free reasoning among equals. Provided that the procedures of the deliberation secure impartiality, equality, openness and lack of coercion, they will guide the deliberation towards generalizable interests which can be agreed by all participants, thereby producing legitimate outcomes. The issue of legitimacy is more heavily stressed by the Habermasians, but there is no fundamental difference between Habermas and Rawls on this question. Indeed Rawls defines the liberal principle of legitimacy in a way which is congruent with Habermas's view: 'Our exercise of political power is proper and hence justifiable only when it is exercised in accordance with a constitution the essentials of which all citizens may reasonably be expected to endorse in the light of principles and ideals acceptable to them as reasonable and rational.'[13] This normative force given to the principle of general justification chimes with Habermas's discourse ethics, and this is why one can certainly argue for the possibility of reformulating Rawlsian political constructivism in the language of discourse ethics.[14] In fact this is to some extent what Cohen does, and this is why he provides a good example of the compatibility between the two approaches. He particularly stresses the deliberative processes and affirms that, when envisaged as a system of social and political arrangements linking the exercise of power to free reasoning among equals, democracy requires the participants not only to be free and equal but also to be 'reasonable'. By this he means that 'they aim to defend and criticize institutions and programs in terms of considerations that others, as free and equal, have *reason to accept*, given the fact of reasonable pluralism'.[15]

THE FLIGHT FROM PLURALISM

After having delineated the main ideas of deliberative democracy, I will now examine in more detail some points of the debate between Rawls and Habermas in view of bringing to the fore what I see as the crucial shortcoming of the deliberative approach. There are two issues which I take as particularly relevant.

The first is that one of the central claims of the 'political liberalism' advocated by Rawls is that it is a liberalism which is political, not metaphysical, and which is independent of comprehensive views. A clear-cut separation is established between the realm of the *private* – where a plurality of different and irreconcilable comprehensive views coexist – and the realm of the *public*, where an overlapping consensus can be established over a shared conception of justice.

Habermas contends that Rawls cannot succeed in his strategy of avoiding philosophically disputed issues, because it is impossible to develop his theory in the freestanding way that he announces. Indeed, his notion of the 'reasonable' as well as his conception of the 'person' necessarily involve him with questions concerning concepts of rationality and truth that he pretends to bypass.[16] Moreover, Habermas declares that his own approach is superior to the Rawlsian one because of its strictly procedural character which allows him to 'leave more questions open because it entrusts more to the *process* of rational opinion and will formation'.[17] By not positing a strong separation between public and private, it is better adapted to accommodate the wide-ranging deliberation that democracy entails. To that, Rawls retorts that Habermas's approach cannot be as strictly procedural as he pretends. It must include a substantive dimension, given that issues concerning the result of the procedures cannot be excluded from their design.[18]

I think that they are both right in their respective criticisms. Indeed, Rawls's conception is not as independent of comprehensive views as he believes, and Habermas cannot be as purely proceduralist as he claims. That both are unable to separate the public from the private or the procedural from the substantial as clearly as they declare is very telling. What this reveals is the impossibility of achieving what each of them, albeit in different ways, is really aiming at, that is, circumscribing a domain that would not be subject to the pluralism of values and where a consensus without exclusion could be established. Indeed, Rawls's avoidance of comprehensive doctrines is motivated by his belief that no rational agreement is possible in this field. This is why, in order for liberal institutions to be acceptable to people with differing moral, philosophical and religious views, they must be neutral with respect to comprehensive views. Hence the strong separation that he tries to install between the realm of the private – with its pluralism of irreconcilable values – and the realm of the public, where a political agreement on a liberal conception of justice would be secured through the creation of an overlapping consensus on justice.

In the case of Habermas a similar attempt of escaping the implications of value pluralism is made through the distinction between *ethics* – a domain which allows for competing conceptions of the good life – and *morality* – a domain where a strict proceduralism can be implemented and impartiality reached leading to the formulation of universal principles. Rawls and Habermas want to ground adhesion to liberal democracy on a type of rational agreement that would preclude the possibility of contestation. This is why they need to relegate pluralism to a non-public domain in order to insulate politics from its consequences. That they are unable to maintain the tight separation they advocate has very important implications for democratic politics. It highlights the fact that the domain of politics – even when fundamental issues like justice or basic principles are concerned – is not a neutral terrain that could be insulated from the pluralism of values and where rational, universal solutions could be formulated.

The second issue is another question that concerns the relation between private autonomy and political autonomy. As we have seen, both authors aim at reconciling the 'liberties of the ancients' with the 'liberties of the moderns' and they argue that the two types of autonomy necessarily go together. However, Habermas considers that only his approach manages to establish the co-originality of individual rights and democratic participation. He affirms that Rawls subordinates democratic sovereignty to liberal rights because he envisages public autonomy as a means to authorize private autonomy. But as Charles Larmore has pointed out, Habermas, for his part, privileges the democratic aspect, since he asserts that the importance of individual rights lies in their making democratic self-government possible.[19] So we have to conclude that, in this case again, neither of them is able to deliver what they announce. What they want to deny is the paradoxical nature of modern democracy and the fundamental tension between the logic of democracy and the logic of liberalism. They are unable to acknowledge that, while it is indeed the case that individual rights and democratic self-government are constitutive of liberal democracy – whose novelty resides precisely in the articulation of those two traditions – there exists between their respective 'grammars' a tension that can never be eliminated. To be sure, contrary to what adversaries like Carl Schmitt have argued, this does not mean that liberal democracy is a doomed regime. Such a tension, though ineradicable, can be negotiated in different ways. Indeed, a great part of democratic politics is precisely about the negotiation of that paradox and the articulation of precarious solutions.[20] What is misguided is the search for a final rational resolution. Not only can it not succeed, but moreover it leads to putting undue constraints on the political debate. Such a search should be recognized for what it really is, another attempt at insulating politics from the effects of the pluralism of value, this time by trying to fix once and for all the meaning and hierarchy of the central liberal-democratic values. Democratic theory should renounce those forms of escapism and face the challenge that the recognition of the pluralism of values entails. This does not mean accepting a total pluralism, and some limits need to be put to the kind of confrontation which is going to be seen as legitimate in the public sphere. But the political nature of the limits should be acknowledged instead of being presented as requirements of morality or rationality.

WHICH ALLEGIANCE FOR DEMOCRACY

If both Rawls and Habermas, albeit in different ways, aim at reaching a form of rational consensus instead of a 'simple modus vivendi' or a 'mere agreement', it is because they believe that, by procuring stable grounds for liberal democracy, such a consensus will contribute to securing the future of liberal-democratic institutions. As we have seen, while Rawls considers that the key issue is justice, for Habermas it has to do with legitimacy. According to Rawls, a well-ordered society is one which functions according to the principles laid down by a shared conception of justice. This is what produces stability and citizens' acceptance of their institutions. For Habermas a stable and well-functioning democracy requires the creation of a polity integrated through rational insight into legitimacy. This is why for the Habermasians the central issue lies in finding a way to guarantee that decisions taken by democratic institutions represent an impartial standpoint expressing equally the interests of all, which requires establishing procedures able to deliver rational results through democratic participation. As put by Seyla Benhabib, 'legitimacy in complex democratic societies must be thought to result from the free and unconstrained public deliberation of all on matters of common concern'.[21]

In their desire to show the limitations of the democratic consensus as envisaged by the aggregative model – only concerned with instrumental rationality and the promotion of self-interest – deliberative democrats insist on the importance of another type of rationality, the rationality at work in communicative action and free public reason. They want to make it the central moving force of democratic citizens and the basis of their allegiance to their common institutions.

Their concern with the current state of democratic institutions is one that I share, but I consider their answer as being profoundly inadequate. The solution to our current predicament does not reside in replacing the dominant 'means–ends rationality' by another form of rationality, a 'deliberative' and 'communicative' one. True, there is space for different understandings of reason and it is important to complexify the picture offered by the holders of the instrumentalist view. However, simply replacing one type of rationality by another is not going to help us address the real problem that the issue of allegiance poses. As Michael Oakeshott has reminded us, the authority of political institutions is not a question of *consent* but of the continuous acknowledgement of *cives* who recognize their obligation to obey the conditions prescribed in *res publica*.[22] Following that line of thought we can realize that what is really at stake in the allegiance to democratic institutions is the constitution of an ensemble of practices that make possible the creation of democratic citizens. This is not a matter of *rational justification* but of *availability* of democratic forms of individuality and subjectivity. By privileging rationality, both the deliberative and the aggregative perspectives leave aside a central element which is the crucial role played by passions and affects in securing allegiance to democratic values. This cannot be ignored, and it entails envisaging the question of democratic citizenship in a very different way. The failure of current democratic theory to tackle the question of citizenship is the consequence of their operating with a conception of the subject which sees individuals as prior to society, bearers of natural rights, and either utility maximizing agents or rational subjects. In all cases they are abstracted from social and power relations, language, culture and the whole set of practices that make agency possible. What is precluded in these rationalistic approaches is the very question of what are the conditions of existence of the democratic subject.

The view that I want to put forward is that it is not by providing arguments about the rationality embodied in liberal-democratic institutions that one can contribute to the creation of democratic citizens. Democratic individuals can only be made possible by multiplying the institutions, the discourses, the forms of life that foster identification with democratic values. This is why, although agreeing with deliberative democrats about the need for a different understanding of democracy, I see their proposals as counterproductive. To be sure, we need to formulate an alternative to the aggregative model and to the instrumentalist conception of politics that it fosters. It has become clear that by discouraging the active involvement of citizens in the running of the polity and by encouraging the privatization of life, they have not secured the stability that they were announcing. Extreme forms of individualism have become widespread which threaten the very social fabric. On the other side, deprived of the possibility of identifying with valuable conceptions of citizenship, many people are increasingly searching for other forms of collective identification, which can very often put into jeopardy the civic bond that should unite a democratic political association. The growth of various religious, moral and ethnic fundamentalisms is, in my view, the direct consequence of the democratic deficit which characterizes most liberal-democratic societies.

To seriously tackle those problems, the only way is to envisage democratic citizenship from a different perspective, one that puts the emphasis on the types of *practices* and not the forms of *argumentation*. In *The Return of the Political*, I have argued that the reflections on civil association developed by Michael Oakeshott in *On Human Conduct* are very pertinent for envisaging the modern form of political community and the type of bond uniting democratic citizens, the specific language of civil intercourse that he calls the *res publica*.[23] But we can also take inspiration from Wittgenstein who, as I have shown,[24] provides very important insights for a critique of rationalism. Indeed in his later work he has highlighted the fact that, in order to have agreement in opinions, there must first be agreement in forms of life. In his view, to agree on the definition of a term is not enough and we need agreement in the way we use it. This means that procedures should be envisaged as a complex ensemble of practices. It is because they are inscribed in shared forms of life and agreements in judgements that procedures can be accepted and followed. They cannot be seen as rules that are created on the basis of principles and then applied to specific cases. Rules for Wittgenstein are always abridgements of practices, they are inseparable from specific forms of life. This indicates that a strict separation between 'procedural' and 'substantial' or between 'moral' and 'ethical', separations which are central to the Habermasian approach, cannot be maintained. Procedures always involve substantial ethical commitments, and there can never be such a thing as purely neutral procedures.

Viewed from such a standpoint, allegiance to democracy and belief in the value of its institutions do not depend on giving them an intellectual foundation. It is more in the nature of what Wittgenstein likens to 'a passionate commitment to a system of reference. Hence, although it's *belief*, it is really a way of living, or of assessing one's life.'[25] Contrary to deliberative democracy, such a perspective also implies, to acknowledge the limits of consensus: 'Where two principles really do meet which cannot be reconciled with one another, then each man declares the other a fool and an heretic. I said I would "combat" the other man, – but wouldn't I give him reasons? Certainly; but how far do they go? At the end of reasons comes persuasion.'[26]

Seeing things in that way should make us realize that taking pluralism seriously requires that we give up the dream of a rational consensus which entails the fantasy that we could escape from our human form of life. In our desire for a total grasp, says Wittgenstein, 'We have got on to the slippery ice where there is no friction and so in a certain sense the conditions are ideal, but also, just because of that, we are unable to walk: so we need *friction*. Back to the rough ground.'[27]

Back to the rough ground here means coming to terms with the fact that, far from being merely empirical or epistemological, the obstacles to rationalist devices like the 'original condition' or 'the ideal discourse' are ontological. Indeed, the free and unconstrained public deliberation of all on matters of common concern is a conceptual impossibility, since the particular forms of life which are presented as its 'impediments' are its very condition of possibility. Without them no communication, no deliberation, would ever take place. There is absolutely no justification for attributing a special privilege to a so-called 'moral point of view' governed by rationality and impartiality and where a rational universal consensus could be reached.

AN 'AGONISTIC' MODEL OF DEMOCRACY

Besides putting the emphasis on practices and language-games, an alternative to the rationalist framework also requires coming to terms with the fact that power is constitutive of social relations. One of the shortcomings of the deliberative approach is that, by postulating the availability of a public sphere where power would have been eliminated and where a rational consensus could be realized, this model of democratic politics is unable to acknowledge the dimension of antagonism that the pluralism of values entails and its ineradicable character. This is why it is bound to miss the specificity of the political which it can only envisage as a specific domain of morality. Deliberative democracy provides a very good illustration of what Carl Schmitt had said about liberal thought: 'In a very systematic fashion liberal thought evades or ignores state and politics and moves instead in a typical always recurring polarity of two heterogeneous spheres, namely ethics and economics.'[28] Indeed, to the aggregative model, inspired by economics, the only alternative deliberative democrats can oppose is one that collapses politics into ethics.

In order to remedy this serious deficiency, we need a democratic model able to grasp the nature of the political. This requires developing an approach which places the question of power and antagonism at its very centre. It is such an approach that I want to advocate and whose theoretical bases have been delineated in *Hegemony and Socialist Strategy*.[29] The central thesis of the book is that social objectivity is constituted through acts of power. This implies that any social objectivity is ultimately political and that it has to show the traces of exclusion which governs its constitution. This point of convergence – or rather mutual collapse – between objectivity and power is what we meant by 'hegemony'. This way of posing the problem indicates that power should not be conceived as an external relation taking place between two preconstituted identities, but rather as constituting the identities themselves. Since any political order is the expression of a hegemony, of a specific pattern of power relations, political practice cannot be envisaged as simply representing the interests of preconstituted identities, but as constituting those identities themselves in a precarious and always vulnerable terrain.

To assert the hegemonic nature of any kind of social order is to operate a displacement of the traditional relation between democracy and power. According to the deliberative approach, the more democratic a society is, the less power would be constitutive of social relations. But if we accept that relations of power are constitutive of the social, then the main question for democratic politics is not how to eliminate power but how to constitute forms of power more compatible with democratic values.

Coming to terms with the constitutive nature of power implies relinquishing the ideal of a democratic society as the realization of a perfect harmony or transparency. The democratic character of a society can only be given by the fact that no limited social actor can attribute to herself or himself the representation of the totality and claim to have the 'mastery' of the foundation.

Democracy requires, therefore, that the purely constructed nature of social relations finds its complement in the purely pragmatic grounds of the claims to power legitimacy. This implies that there is no unbridgeable gap between power and legitimacy – not obviously in the sense that all power is automatically legitimate, but in the sense that: (a) if any power has been able to impose itself, it is because it has been recognized as legitimate in some quarters; and (b) if legitimacy is not based in an aprioristic ground, it is because it is based in some form of successful power. This link between legitimacy and power and the hegemonic ordering that this entails is precisely what the deliberative approach forecloses by positing the possibility of a type of rational argumentation where power has been eliminated and where legitimacy is grounded on pure rationality.

Once the theoretical terrain has been delineated in such a way, we can begin formulating an alternative to both the aggregative and the deliberative model, one that I propose to call 'agonistic pluralism'.[30] A first distinction is needed in order to clarify the new perspective that I am putting forward, the distinction between 'politics' and 'the political'. By 'the political', I refer to the dimension of antagonism that is inherent in human relations, antagonism that can take many forms and emerge in different types of social relations. 'Politics', on the other side, indicates the ensemble of practices, discourses and institutions which seek to establish a certain order and organize human coexistence in conditions that are always potentially conflictual because they are affected by the dimension of 'the political'. I consider that it is only when we acknowledge the dimension of 'the political' and understand that 'politics' consists in domesticating hostility and in trying to defuse the potential antagonism that exists in human relations, that we can pose what I take to be the central question for democratic politics. This question, pace the rationalists, is not how to arrive at a consensus without exclusion, since this would imply the eradication of the political. Politics aims at the creation of unity in a context of conflict and diversity; it is always concerned with the creation of an 'us' by the determination of a 'them'. The novelty of democratic politics is not the overcoming of this us/them opposition – which is an impossibility – but the different way in which it is established. The crucial issue is to establish this us/them discrimination in a way that is compatible with pluralist democracy.

Envisaged from the point of view of 'agonistic pluralism', the aim of democratic politics is to construct the 'them' in such a way that it is no longer perceived as an enemy to be destroyed, but as an 'adversary', that is, somebody whose ideas we combat but whose right to defend those ideas we do not put into question. This is the real meaning of liberal-democratic tolerance, which does not entail condoning ideas that we oppose or being indifferent to standpoints that we disagree with, but treating those who defend them as legitimate opponents. This category of the 'adversary' does not eliminate antagonism, though, and it should be distinguished from the liberal notion of the competitor with which it is sometimes identified. An adversary is an enemy, but a legitimate enemy, one with whom we have some common ground because we have a shared adhesion to the ethico-political principles of liberal democracy: liberty and equality. But we disagree concerning the meaning and implementation of those principles, and such a disagreement is not one that could be resolved through deliberation and rational discussion. Indeed, given the ineradicable pluralism of value, there is no rational resolution of the conflict, hence its antagonistic dimension.[31] This does not mean, of course, that adversaries can never cease to disagree, but that does not prove that antagonism has been eradicated. To accept the view of the adversary is to undergo a radical change in political identity. It is more a sort of *conversion* than a process of rational persuasion (in the same way as Thomas Kuhn has argued that adherence to a new scientific paradigm is a conversion). Compromises are, of course, also possible; they are part and parcel of politics; but they should be seen as temporary respites in an ongoing confrontation.

Introducing the category of the 'adversary' requires complexifying the notion of antagonism and distinguishing two different forms in which it can emerge, *antagonism* properly speaking and *agonism*. *Antagonism* is struggle between enemies, while *agonism* is struggle between adversaries. We can therefore reformulate our problem by saying that envisaged from the perspective of 'agonistic pluralism' the aim of democratic politics is to transform *antagonism* into *agonism*. This requires providing channels through which collective passions will be given ways to express themselves over issues which, while allowing enough possibility for identification, will not construct the opponent as an enemy but as an adversary. An important difference with the model of 'deliberative democracy' is that for 'agonistic pluralism', the prime task of democratic politics is not to eliminate passions from the sphere of the public, in order to render a rational consensus possible, but to mobilize those passions towards democratic designs.

One of the keys to the thesis of agonistic pluralism is that, far from jeopardizing democracy, agonistic confrontation is in fact its very condition of existence. Modern democracy's specificity lies in the recognition and legitimation of conflict and the refusal to suppress it by imposing an authoritarian order. Breaking with the symbolic representation of society as an organic body – which was characteristic of the holist mode of social organization – a democratic society acknowledges the pluralism of values, the 'disenchantment of the world' diagnosed by Max Weber and the unavoidable conflicts that it entails.

I agree with those who affirm that a pluralist democracy demands a certain amount of consensus and that it requires allegiance to the values which constitute its 'ethico-political principles'. But since those ethico-political principles can only exist through many different and conflicting interpretations, such a consensus is bound to be a 'conflictual consensus'. This is indeed the privileged terrain of agonistic confrontation among adversaries. Ideally such a confrontation should be staged around the diverse conceptions of citizenship which correspond to the different interpretations of the ethico-political principles: liberal-conservative, social-democratic, neo-liberal, radical-democratic, and so on. Each of them proposes its own interpretation of the 'common good', and tries to implement a different form of hegemony. To foster allegiance to its institutions, a democratic system requires the availability of those contending forms of citizenship identification. They provide the terrain in which passions can be mobilized around democratic objectives and antagonism transformed into agonism.

A well-functioning democracy calls for a vibrant clash of democratic political positions. If this is missing there is the danger that this democratic confrontation will be replaced by a confrontation among other forms of collective identification, as is the case with identity politics. Too much emphasis on consensus and the refusal of confrontation lead to apathy and disaffection with political participation. Worse still, the result can be the crystallization of collective passions around issues which cannot be managed by the democratic process and an explosion of antagonisms that can tear up the very basis of civility.

It is for that reason that the ideal of a pluralist democracy cannot be to reach a rational consensus in the public sphere. Such a consensus cannot exist. We have to accept that every consensus exists as a temporary result of a provisional hegemony, as a stabilization of power, and that it always entails some form of exclusion. The ideas that power could be dissolved through a rational debate and that legitimacy could be based on pure rationality are illusions which can endanger democratic institutions.

What the deliberative-democracy model is denying is the

dimension of undecidability and the ineradicability of antagon-ism which are constitutive of the political. By postulating the availability of a non-exclusive public sphere of deliberation where a rational consensus could obtain, they negate the inherently conflictual nature of modern pluralism. They are unable to recognize that bringing a deliberation to a close always results from a *decision* which excludes other possibilities and for which one should never refuse to bear responsibility by invoking the commands of general rules or principles. This is why a perspec-tive like 'agonistic pluralism', which reveals the impossibility of establishing a consensus without exclusion, is of fundamental importance for democratic politics. By warning us against the illusion that a fully achieved democracy could ever be instan-tiated, it forces us to keep the democratic contestation alive. To make room for dissent and to foster the institutions in which it can be manifested is vital for a pluralist democracy, and one should abandon the very idea that there could ever be a time in which it would cease to be necessary because the society is now 'well-ordered'. An 'agonistic' approach acknowledges the real nature of its frontiers and the forms of exclusion that they entail, instead of trying to disguise them under the veil of rationality or morality. Coming to terms with the hegemonic nature of social relations and identities, it can contribute to subverting the ever-present temptation existing in democratic societies to naturalize its frontiers and essentialize its identities. For this reason it is much more receptive than the deliberative model to the multi-plicity of voices that contemporary pluralist societies encompass and to the complexity of their power structure.

NOTES

1. Joseph Schumpeter, *Capitalism, Socialism and Democracy*, New York, 1947.

2. Anthony Downs, *An Economic Theory of Democracy*, New York, 1957.

3. John Rawls, *A Theory of Justice* , Cambridge, MA, 1974.

4. See for instance Jürgen Habermas, 'Three Normative Models of Democracy', in Seyla Benhabib (ed.), *Democracy and Difference*, Princeton, 1966, p. 29.

5. John Rawls, *Political Liberalism*, New York, 1993, p. 5.

6. Jürgen Habermas, *Between Facts and Norms: Contributions to a Discourse Theory of Law and Democracy*, Cambridge, MA, 1996, p. 127.

7. Joshua Cohen, 'Democracy and Liberty', in J. Elster (ed.), *Deliberative Democracy*, Cambridge, 1988, p. 187.

8. Seyla Benhabib, 'Toward a Deliberative Model of Democratic Legitimacy', in Seyla Benhabib (ed.), *Democracy and Difference*, Princeton, 1996, p. 77.

9. Benhabib, 'Toward a Deliberative Model', p. 70.

10. Cohen, 'Democracy and Liberty', p. 186.

11. Benhabib, 'Toward a Deliberative Model', p. 69.

12. Jürgen Habermas, 'Further Reflections on the Public Sphere', in C. Calhoun (ed.), *Habermas and the Public Sphere*, Cambridge, MA, 1991, p. 448.

13. Rawls, *Political Liberalism*, p. 217.

14. Such an argument is made by Rainer Forst in his review of 'Political Liberalism' in *Constellations* 1, 1, p. 169.

15. Cohen, 'Democracy and Liberty', p. 194.

16. Jürgen Habermas, 'Reconciliation Through the Public Use of Reason: Remarks on John Rawls's Political Liberalism', *The Journal of Philosophy* XXCII, 3, 1995, p. 126.

17. Ibid., p. 131.

18. John Rawls, 'Reply to Habermas', *The Journal of Philosophy* XCII, 3, 1995, pp. 170–74.

19. Charles Larmore, *The Morals of Modernity*, Cambridge, 1996, p. 217.

20. I have developed this argument in my article 'Carl Schmitt and the Paradox of Liberal Democracy', in Chantal Mouffe (ed.), *The Challenge of Carl Schmitt*, London, 1999; also Chapter 2, this volume.

21. Benhabib, 'Toward a Deliberative Model', pp. 68.

22. Michael Oakeshott, *On Human Conduct*, Oxford, 1975, pp. 149–58.

23. Chantal Mouffe, *The Return of the Political*, London, 1993, Chapter 4.

24. See 'Wittgenstein, Political Theory and Democracy', Chapter 3, this volume.

25. Ludwig Wittgenstein, *Culture and Value*, Chicago, 1980, p. 85e

26. Ludwig Wittgenstein, *On Certainty*, New York, 1969, p. 81e.

27. Ludwig Wittgenstein, *Philosophical Investigations*, Oxford, 1958, p. 46e.

28. Carl Schmitt, *The Concept of the Political*, New Brunswick, 1976, p. 70.

29. Ernesto Laclau and Chantal Mouffe, *Hegemony and Socialist Strategy: Towards a Radical Democratic Politics*, London, 1985.

30. 'Agonistic pluralism' as defined here is an attempt to operate what Richard Rorty would call a 'redescription' of the basic self-understanding of the liberal-democratic regime, one which stresses the importance of acknowledging its conflictual dimension. It therefore needs to be distinguished from the way the same term is used by John Gray to refer to the larger rivalry between whole forms of life which he sees as 'the deeper truth of which agonistic liberalism is only one exemplar'. In John Gray, *Enlightenment's Wake: Politics and Culture at the Close of the Modern Age*, London, 1995, p. 84.

31. This antagonistic dimension, which can never be completely eliminated but only 'tamed' or 'sublimated' by being, so to speak, 'played out' in an agonistic way, is what, in my view, distinguishes my understanding of agonism from the one put forward by other 'agonistic theorists', those who are influenced by Nietzsche or Hannah Arendt, like William Connolly or Bonnie Honig. It seems to me that their conception leaves open the possibility that the political could under certain conditions be made absolutely congruent with the ethical, optimism which I do not share.

5

A POLITICS WITHOUT ADVERSARY?

Since the mid-1980s – and this was of course accelerated by the collapse of communism – we have heard a lot about the demise of the left/right opposition, and this has been accompanied by a move towards the centre of most socialist parties. Since New Labour came to power in Britain such a move is presented as the new form of radicalism, the cornerstone of a politics coming to terms with the 'death of socialism' and the 'challenge of globalization'. After promoting the label of 'centre-left', Blair and his advisers now generally try avoiding any reference to the left altogether. Since its victory New Labour has begun to market itself as a radical movement, albeit of a new type, a third way between social democracy and neo-liberalism. This third way, marketed by Tony Blair as the 'New Politics for the New Century' in a Fabian Pamphlet, is envisaged as occupying a position which, by being located *above* left and right, thereby manages to overcome their old antagonism. Unlike the traditional centre, which lies in the middle of the spectrum between right and left, this, we are told, is a 'radical centre' that transcends the traditional left/right division by articulating themes and values from both sides in a new synthesis.

An attempt to theorize this supposedly new model for progressive politics has been made by Anthony Giddens in two books: *Beyond Left and Right* and, more recently, *The Third Way*.[1] Socialism, argues Giddens, is dead, and this is true not only for its communist but also for its traditional social-democratic version whose aim was to confront the limitations of capitalism in order to humanize it. But social democracy under-estimated the capacity for capitalism to adapt and innovate. Moreover, it was based on a 'cybernetic model' of social life which could make sense in a world of 'simple modernization' but cannot work any more in a globalized, post-traditional social order characterized by the expansion of social reflexivity. In today's world of 'reflexive modernization' we need, he says, a new type of radical politics because life politics are now more important than life chance politics. The alternative to state action is a 'generative' politics that provides a framework for the life-political decisions of the individual and allows people to make things happen themselves. Democracy should become 'dialogic', and far from being limited to the political sphere, it has to reach the various areas of personal life, aiming at a 'democracy of the emotions'. This new 'life' politics overcomes the traditional left/right divide, since it draws on philosophic conservatism while preserving some of the core values usually associated with socialism.

It is worth noting that since he wrote *Beyond Left and Right*, Giddens's position has slightly shifted. He seems to have realized that it was not good political strategy to dismiss the social-democratic tradition completely, and his more recent book, *The Third Way*, is subtitled 'The Renewal of Social Democracy'. This is no doubt progress, but the problem is that the proposed 'renewal' consists in fact of draining the social-democratic pro-ject of its anti-capitalist component. Such a move is of course consistent with his main agenda of delineating a 'win–win politics' that goes beyond the adversarial model by promoting solutions that supposedly benefit all people in society. But this is precisely where the fundamental flaw of this supposedly new form of radicalism lies.

Let me make clear at the outset that the problem I see in this notion of the radical centre is not its rejection of traditional left solutions. The critique of statism and productivism is far from new and many people who still identify with the left have long been aware of the shortcomings of social democracy. The problem is not in the third way embracing some conservative themes either. The postmodern critique of Enlightenment epistemology – from which Giddens is at pains to dissociate himself – has for some time already stressed the possibility and the need to dissociate the left project from its rationalistic premises. Several attempts to reformulate the aims of the left in terms of 'radical and plural democracy' have pointed out how, by helping us to problematize the idea of progress inherited from the Enlightenment, some themes developed by traditional conservative philosophers could contribute to the elaboration of a radical politics.

What is really the problem with the advocates of the 'radical centre' is, I believe, their claim that a left/right divide, a heritage of 'simple modernization', is not relevant any more in times of 'reflexive modernization'. By asserting that a radical politics today should transcend this divide and conceive democratic life as a dialogue, they imply that we now live in a society which is no longer structured by social division. Nowadays politics operates supposedly on a neutral terrain and solutions are available that could satisfy everybody. Relations of power and their constitutive role in society are obliterated and the conflicts that they entail reduced to a simple competition of interests that can be harmonized through dialogue. This is the typical liberal perspective that envisages democracy as a competition among elites, making adversary forces invisible and reducing politics to an exchange of arguments and the negotiation of compromises. I submit that to present such a view of politics as 'radical' is really disingenuous, and that instead of being conducive to more democracy the radical centrism advocated by New Labour is in fact a renunciation of the basic tenets of radical politics.

The central flaw of the attempt to modernize social democracy by third way theorists is that it is based on the illusion that, by not defining an adversary, one can side-step fundamental conflicts of interests. Social democrats never made that mistake. As Mike Rustin points out, social democracy, in both its right- and left-wing variants, always had capitalism as one of its antagonists, and its task was to confront holistically the sytemic problems of inequality and instability generated by capitalism.[2] The third way approach, on the contrary, is unable to grasp the systemic connections existing between global market forces and the variety of problems – from exclusion to environmental risks – that it pretends to tackle.

Indeed, the main shortcoming of Giddens's analysis is that he appears to be unaware of the drastic measures that would be required to put most of his proposals into practice. It is all very nice to announce that there should be 'no rights without responsibilities' or 'no authority without democracy', but how is one going to put such programmes into practice without profoundly challenging the existing structures of power and authority? Without calling for the sort of total overthrow of capitalism advocated by some Marxists, one can surely acknowledge that some form of anti-capitalist struggle cannot be eliminated from a radical politics aiming at the democratization of society, and that without the transformation of the prevalent hegemonic configuration little change will be possible.

As Alan Ryan, among others, has pointed out, there is a genuine hole at the heart of Labour policy because having abandoned the idea that the ownership of the means of production was a central issue in politics, they have not been able to put anything else at that place.[3] Hence the shallowness of their economic strategy. They believe that setting moral agendas for remoralizing the poor and preparing people for 'flexibility' will be enough to create the good inclusive society whose values they are preaching. Indeed, the joint declaration in which Blair and Schröder delineate their view of the third way for Europe, besides laying out a programme of deregulation and tax reductions tempered by state intervention to provide education and training, stresses the need to end conflicts at the workplace and calls for a spirit of community and solidarity in order to strengthen dialogue between all groups in society.

No wonder that within such a perspective there is no room for properly feminist demands since, as Anna Coote has shown, they do not fit into Blair's vision of a pain-free politics for middle England.[4] For women to increase their political strength would require men to give up some of theirs. But, she states, New Labour is not prepared to accommodate a zero-sum game; it wants no losers, especially among middle England voters. Moreover, it is led by a closed circle of elite white males who enjoy power and do not want to give it up.

CONFLICT AND MODERN DEMOCRACY

New Labour represents the clearer example of the 'Clintoniza-tion' of European social democracy, but as the recent joint British–German declaration testifies, the signs of the third way virus are present elsewhere and the disease might be spreading. Its roots are to be found in the fact that the coming to terms by the left with the importance of pluralism and of liberal-democratic institutions has been accompanied by the mistaken belief that this meant abandoning any attempt to offer an alternative to the present hegemonic order. Hence the sacraliza-tion of consensus, the blurring of the left/right distinction and the present urge of many left parties to locate themselves at the centre.

But this is to miss a crucial point, not only about the primary reality of strife in social life, but also about the integra-tive role that conflict plays in modern democracy. As I have argued through these essays, the specificity of modern democ-racy lies in the recognition and the legitimation of conflict and the refusal to suppress it through the imposition of an authori-tarian order. A well-functioning democracy calls for a confron-tation between democratic political positions, and this requires a real debate about possible alternatives. Consensus is indeed necessary but it must be accompanied by dissent. There is no contradiction in saying that, as some would pretend. Consensus is needed on the institutions which are constitutive of democ-racy. But there will always be disagreement concerning the way social justice should be implemented in these institutions. In a pluralist democracy such a disagreement should be considered as legitimate and indeed welcome. We can agree on the import-ance of 'liberty and equality for all', while disagreeing sharply about their meaning and the way they should be implemented, with the different configurations of power relations that this implies. It is precisely this kind of disagreement which provides the stuff of democratic politics and it is what the struggle between left and right should be about. This is why, instead of relinquishing them as outdated, we should redefine those categories. When political frontiers become blurred, the dynamics of politics is obstructed and the constitution of distinctive political identities is hindered. Disaffection towards political parties sets in and it discourages participation in the political process. Alas, as we have begun to witness in many countries, the result is not a more mature, reconciled society without sharp divisions but the growth of other types of collective identities around religious, nationalist or ethnic forms of identification. In other words, when democratic confrontation disappears, the political in its antagonistic dimension manifests itself through other channels. Antagonisms can take many forms and it is illusory to believe that they could ever be eliminated. This is why it is preferable to give them a political outlet within an 'agonistic' pluralistic democratic system.

The deplorable spectacle provided by the USA with the trivialization of political stakes provides a good example of the degeneration of the democratic public sphere. Clinton's sexual saga was a direct consequence of this new kind of bland, homogenized political world resulting from the effects of his strategy of triangulation. Sure, it allowed him to gain a second term by neutralizing his adversaries thanks to skilfully drawing on republican ideas that resonated with voters and articulating them with leftist policies on abortion and education. But at the cost of further impoverishing an already weak political public sphere. One should realize that a lack of democratic contestation over real political alternatives leads to antagonisms manifesting themselves under forms that undermine the very basis of the democratic public sphere. The development of a moralistic discourse and the obsessive unveiling of scandals in all realms of life, as well as the growth of various types of religious fundamentalism, are too often the consequence of the void created in political life by the absence of democratic forms of identification informed by competing political values.

Clearly the problem is not limited to the United States. A look at other countries where, because of different traditions, the sexual card cannot be played in the same way as in the Anglo-American world shows that the crusade against corruption and shabby deals can play a similar role in replacing the missing political line of demarcation between adversaries. In other circumstances yet, the political frontier might be drawn around religious identities or around non-negotiable moral values, as in the case of abortion, but in all cases what this reveals is a democratic deficit created by the blurring of the left/right divide and the trivialization of the political discourse.

It is also in the context of the weakening of the democratic political public sphere where an agonistic confrontation could take place that the increasing dominance of the juridical level should be understood. Given the growing impossibility of envisaging the problems of society in a properly political way, there is a marked tendency to privilege the juridical field and to expect the law to provide the solutions to all types of conflict. The juridical sphere is becoming the terrain where social conflicts can find a form of expression, and the legal system is seen as responsible for organizing human coexistence and for regulating social relations. With the blurring of the left/right divide, liberal-democratic societies have lost the capacity to symbolically order social relations in a political way and to give form to the decisions they have to face through political discourses.

The current hegemony of juridical discourse is defended and theorized by people like Ronald Dworkin, who asserts the primacy of the independent judiciary, presented as the interpreter of the political morality of a community. According to Dworkin, the fundamental questions facing a political community in the fields of unemployment, education, censorship, freedom of association, and so forth, are better resolved by the judges, providing that they interpret the constitution by reference to the principle of political equality. Very little is left for the political arena.

Another, even more worrying consequence of the democratic deficit linked to the obsession with centrist politics is the increasing role played by populist right-wing parties. Indeed, I submit that the rise of this type of party should be understood in the context of the 'consensus at the centre' form of politics which allows populist parties challenging the dominant consensus to appear as the only anti-Establishment forces representing the will of the people. Thanks to a clever populist rhetoric, they are able to articulate many demands of the popular sectors scorned as retrograde by the modernizing elites and to present themselves as the only guarantors of the sovereignty of the people. Such a situation, I believe, would not have been possible had more real political choices been available within the traditional democratic spectrum.

POLITICS AND THE POLITICAL

Unfortunately the dominant approach in political theory, dominated as it is by a rationalistic and individualistic perspective, is completely unable to help us understand what is happening. This is why, against the two dominant models of democratic politics, the 'aggregative' one that reduces it to the negotiation of interests and the 'deliberative' or 'dialogic' one which believes that decisions on matters of common concern should result from the free and unconstrained public deliberation of all, I have proposed to envisage democratic politics as a form of 'agonistic pluralism' in order to stress that in modern democratic politics, the crucial problem is how to transform *antagonism* into *agonism*. In my view the aim of democratic politics should be to provide the framework through which conflicts can take the form of an agonistic confrontation among adversaries instead of manifesting themselves as an antagonistic struggle between enemies.

I consider that the shortcomings of third way politics help us to understand why envisaging modern democracy as a form of agonistic pluralism has very important consequences for politics. Once it is acknowledged that this type of agonistic confrontation is what is specific to a pluralist democracy, we can understand why such a democracy requires the creation of collective identities around clearly differentiated positions as well as the possibility to choose between real alternatives. This is precisely the function of the left/right distinction. The left/right opposition is the way in which legitimate conflict is given form and institutionalized. If this framework does not exist or is weakened, the process of transformation of antagonism into agonism is hindered, and this can have dire consequences for democracy. This is why discourses about the 'end of politics' and the irrelevance of the left/right distinction should be cause not for celebration but for concern. To be sure, the traditional framework is in dire need of overhauling and it is not a question of reasserting the old slogans and the dogmatic certainties. But it would be a mistake to believe that such a distinction could be transcended and that a radical politics could exist without defining an adversary.

PROBLEMATIZING GLOBALIZATION

Those who argue for the need to go beyond right and left affirm that in the type of globalizing, reflexive society in which we live, neither conservatism nor socialism can provide adequate solutions. No doubt, this is the case. Moreover, it is also true that in political practice the categories of left and right have become increasingly blurred. But to infer from that empirical fact a thesis concerning the necessary irrelevance of such a distinction or to make a value judgement about the desirability of its disappearance is another matter. This might make sense from the perspective of a liberal approach unable to recognize the constitutive role of relations of power and the ineradicability of antagonism; but for those who aim at formulating a progressive politics it is necessary to acknowledge the dimension of what I have proposed to call 'the political' and the impossibility of a reconciled society. Our task should be to redefine the left in order to reactivate the democratic struggle, not to proclaim its obsolescence.

There is in advanced democratic societies an urgent need to re-establish the centrality of politics, and this requires drawing new political frontiers capable of giving a real impulse to democracy. One of the crucial stakes for left democratic politics is to begin providing an alternative to neo-liberalism. It is the current unchallenged hegemony of the neo-liberal discourse which explains why the left is without any credible project. Paradoxically, while increasingly victorious politically – since it is in power in many European countries – the left is still thoroughly defeated ideologically. This is why, despite all the hype about the 'third way', it is unable to take the intellectual initiative. Instead of trying to build a new hegemony, it has capitulated to the neo-liberal one. Hence the 'Thatcherism with a human face' which is the trademark of New Labour.

The usual justification for the 'there is no alternative' dogma is globalization. Indeed, the argument more often rehearsed against redistributive type social-democratic policies is that the tight fiscal restraints faced by the government are the only realistic possibility in a world where voters refuse to pay more taxes and where global markets would not allow any deviation from neo-liberal orthodoxy. This kind of argument takes for granted the ideological terrain which has been established as a result of years of neo-liberal hegemony and transforms what is a circumstantial state of affairs into a historical necessity. Here, as in many other cases, the mantra of globalization is invoked to justify the status quo and reinforce the power of big transnational corporations.[5]

When it is presented as driven exclusively by the information revolution, globalization is deprived of its political dimension and appears as a fate to which we all have to submit. This is precisely where our critique should begin. Scrutinizing this conception, André Gorz has argued that, instead of being seen as the necessary consequence of a technological revolution, the process of globalization must be understood as a move by capital to provide what was a fundamentally political answer to the 'crisis of governability' of the 1970s. In his view, the crisis of the Fordist model of development led to a divorce between the interests of capital and those of the nation-states.[6] The space of politics became dissociated from the space of the economy. To be sure, this phenomenon of globalization was made possible by new forms of technology. But this technical revolution required for its implementation a profound transformation in the relations of power among social groups and between capitalist corporations and the state. The political move was the crucial one. The result is that today corporations have gained a sort of extraterritoriality. They have managed to emancipate themselves from political power and appear as the real locus of sovereignty. It is not surprising that the resources needed to finance the welfare state are diminishing, since the states are unable to tax the transnational corporations.

By unveiling the strategies of power that have informed the process of globalization, Gorz's approach allows us to see the possibility for a counter-strategy. It is of course vain simply to refuse globalization or to attempt resisting it in the context of the nation-state. It is only by opposing to the power of transnational capital another globalization, informed by a different political project, that we could have a chance to resist neo-liberalism succesfully and to instate a new hegemony.

However, such a counter-hegemonic strategy is precisely what is precluded by the very idea of a radical centrism which denies the existence of antagonisms and the need for political frontiers and which proclaims that 'flexibility' is a modern social-democratic aim. To believe that one can accommodate the aims of the big corporations with those of the weaker sectors is already to have capitulated to their power. It is to have accepted their globalization as the only possible one and to act within the constraints that capital is imposing on national governments. The holders of such a view see politics as a game in which everybody could win and where the demands of all could be met without anybody having to lose. For the radical centre, as we have seen, there is of course neither enemy nor adversary. Everybody is part of 'the people'. The interests of the rich transnational corporations can be happily reconciled with those of the unemployed, single mothers and the disabled. Social cohesion is to be secured not through equality, solidarity and an effective exercise of citizenship but through strong families and shared moral values and recognition of duties.

By not leaving any space for the adversarial agonistic contestation of shared values, this new politics of behaviour, which Nikolas Rose calls 'etho-politics', exacerbates the authoritarianism and the social conservatism latent in the communitarian approach.[7] No wonder that New Labour is unable to tolerate the expression of dissent whose expression it sees as a threat to its very existence. However, this politics without an adversary backfires. By pretending to include everybody in 'the people', New Labour contributes to reproducing the subordination of the very people that it is supposed to represent and defend.

THE LEFT AND EQUALITY

Radical politics cannot be located at the centre because to be radical – as Margaret Thatcher, unlike Tony Blair, very well knew – is to aim at a profound transformation of power relations. This cannot be done without drawing political frontiers and defining an adversary or even an enemy. Of course a radical project cannot be successful without winning over a wide variety of sectors. All significant victories of the left have always been the result of an alliance with important sectors of the middle classes whose interests have been articulated to those of the popular sectors. Today more than ever such an alliance is vital for the formulation of a radical project. But this does not mean that such an alliance requires taking the middle ground and trying to establish a compromise between neo-liberalism and the groups that it oppresses. There are many issues concerning the provision of decent public services and the creation of good conditions of life on which a broad alliance could be established. However, this cannot take place without the elaboration of a new hegemonic project that would put again on the agenda the struggle for equality which has been discarded by the advocates of neo-liberalism.

Perhaps the clearest sign of New Labour's renunciation of its left identity is that it has abandoned such a struggle for equality. Under the pretence of formulating a modern, post-social-democratic conception of equality, Blairites have eschewed the language of redistribution in order to speak exclusively in terms of inclusion and exclusion. In their view, the majority of people belong to the middle classes: the only exceptions are a small elite of very rich on one side, and those who are 'excluded' on the other. This new social structure is what provides the basis for the 'consensus at the centre' that they are advocating. Here again we can see that their main tenet is that society is no longer structured through unequal power relations. By redefining the structural inequalities systematically produced by the market system in terms of 'exclusion' they eschew any type of structural analysis of their causes and side-step the fundamental question of what needs to be done to tackle them. As if the very condition for inclusion of the excluded did not require at the very least a new mode of regulation of capitalism which will permit a drastic redistribution and a correction of the profound inequalities which the neo-liberal long decade has brought about.

The current avoidance by New Labour of the theme of

equality and its increasing acceptance of inequalities is very symptomatic indeed. As Norberto Bobbio reminds us, it is the idea of equality which provides the backbone of the left vision while the right – in the name of liberty – has always condoned diverse forms of inequality. The fact that a certain type of egalitarian ideology has been used to justify totalitarian forms of politics in no way forces us to relinquish the struggle for equality. What a left-wing project today requires is to envisage this struggle for equality that has always been at the core of social democracy in a way that takes account of the multiplicity of social relations in which inequality needs to be challenged.

It is not my intention here to defend traditional social democracy and to pretend that it provides the solution. If Thatcherism was successful it is in part because it was able to rearticulate in its favour the popular resentment against the shortcomings of social democracy. The deficiencies of traditional social democracy were due to their lack of understanding of the forms of subordination which were not principally of an economic nature. This is why the emergence of the new social movements were a defining moment in the crisis of the social-democratic model. In many countries this favoured the right, which was able to take advantage of that crisis to mobilize support for the neo-liberal backlash against the welfare state. It would be foolish to believe, therefore, that the solution to our current problems could be the return to a Keynesian social-democratic model, even when envisaged at the European level. What we need today is some form of 'post-social-democratic politics', on condition that this does not mean regressing *behind* social democracy to some pre-social-democratic liberal view but going further towards a more radical and pluralist type of democracy. Yet this type of regression appears to be precisely the kind of move that is behind the logic of many policies – like welfare to work – advocated by the third way. To tackle the multiplicity of forms of subordination existing in social relations, about gender, race, environment and sexuality, a post-social-democratic politics needs to be envisaged in terms of 'radical and plural democracy', as the extension of the struggle for equality and liberty in a wide range of social relations.

John Gray, a long-time critic of social democracy, celebrates New Labour for having abandoned a redistributive, social-democratic idea of justice but worries that they have not put anything in its place. He urges them to reinvent liberal Britain by embracing the New Liberalism advocated in the early decades of the twentieth century by L. T. Hobhouse and T. H. Green. According to such a liberalism, says Gray, economic inequalities were not unfair and the important issue was to reconcile the demands of individual choice with the needs for social cohesion.

I consider that Gray establishes a false dichotomy between equality and individual freedom. To be sure, there will always be a tension between those values, and it is vain to believe that they could be perfectly reconciled. But it does not mean that we should not try to further them both and that we have to discard one to pursue the other. For those who still identify with the left there are ways to envisage social justice which is committed to both pluralism and equality. For instance in *Spheres of Justice* Michael Walzer elaborates such a conception, which he calls 'complex equality'.[8] He argues that if one wants to make equality a central objective of a politics that also respects liberty it is necessary to abandon the idea of 'simple equality', which tends to render people as equal as possible in all areas. Equality in his view is not a simple but a complex relationship between persons mediated by a series of social goods; it does not consist in an identity of possession. According to the complex view of equality that he advocates, social goods should be distributed, not in a uniform manner but in terms of a diversity of criteria which reflect the diversity of those social goods and the meaning attached to them. The important thing is not to violate the principles of distribution proper to each sphere and to preclude success in one sphere implying the possibility of exercising preponderance in others, as is now the case with wealth. It is essential in such a view that no social good be used as the means of domination and that concentration of political power, wealth, honour and offices in the same hands should be avoided. Thinking along those lines could allow New Labour to envisage the struggle against inequality in a way that respects and deepens pluralism instead of stifling individual freedom.

A NEW LEFT-WING PROJECT

The central problem that a post-social-democratic vision informed by a view of complex equality will have to tackle is the crucial transformation with which our societies are confronted: the crisis of work and the exhaustion of the wage society. In this area, more than any other perhaps, it is evident that we have entered a quite different world in which neither laissez-faire liberalism nor Keynesianism will be able to provide a solution. The problem of unemployment does indeed call for new radical thinking. Without realizing that there is no coming back to full employment (if that ever existed) and that a new model of economic development is urgently needed, no alternative to neo-liberalism will ever take off. The Americanization of Europe will proceed under the liberal motto of 'flexibalization'.

A truly radical project needs to start by acknowledging that, as a consequence of the information revolution, there is a growing dissociation between the production of wealth and the quantity of work spent in producing it. Without a drastic redistribution in the average effective duration of work, society will become increasingly polarized between those who work in stable, regular jobs and the rest who are either unemployed or have part-time, precarious and unprotected jobs. In order to fight against such a polarization a series of measures have been proposed which can be roughly summarized in three central points:[9]

1. A significant reduction of the legal and effective duration of the time spent working combined with a politics of active redistribution among salaried employees.
2. The encouragement of a massive development of many non-profit activities by associations, interacting with both the private and the public economies, to provide for the emergence of a truly pluralistic economy, instead of a purely market one.
3. The ending of stigmatization of the poorest and excluded sections of society by the allocation of an unconditional minimum income (basic income) either to every person who does not enjoy the minimum level of resources, or without regard to other income, age, sex or matrimonial status. In both cases this basic income should be made in addition to (and not substitutive for) complementary resources.

Such measures would foment a plural economy where the associative sector would play an important role alongside the market and the state sector. Many activities of crucial social utility discarded by the logic of the market could, through public financing, be carried out in this solidaristic economy. A condition for the success of such initiatives is of course the third measure, the implementation of some form of citizen income that would guarantee a decent minimum for everybody. Clearly, to envisage the different modalities of such an income would be a much better way to approach the reform of the welfare state than replacing it by workfare.

Implemented together, these three sets of measures could create the basis for a post-social-democratic answer to neo-liberalism. Of course such an answer can only be carried out successfully in a European context, and this is why a left-wing project today can only be a European one. In this time of globalization the taming of capitalism cannot be realized at the mere level of the nation-state. Only within the context of an integrated Europe, in which the different states would unite their forces, could the attempt to make finance capital more accountable succeed. If, instead of competing among themselves in order to establish the more attractive deals for transnational corporations, the different European states would agree on common policies, another type of globalization could be possible.

That the traditional conceptions of both the left and the right are inadequate for the problems that we are facing at the eve of the new millennium is something that I readily accept. But to believe that the antagonisms that those categories evoke have disappeared in our globalized world is to fall prey to the hegemonic neo-liberal discourse of the end of politics. Far from having lost their relevance, the stakes to which the left and the right allude are more pertinent than ever. The task ahead is to provide them with a content through which political passions could be redirected towards the democratic agonistic struggle.

NOTES

1. Anthony Giddens, *Beyond Left and Right*, Cambridge, 1994 and *The Third Way*, Cambridge, 1998.

2. Mike Rustin, 'Editorial', *Soundings*, 11, Spring 1999, p. 8.

3. Alan Ryan, 'Britain: Recycling the Third Way', *Dissent*, Spring 1999, p. 79.

4. Anna Coote, 'It's lads on top at Number Ten', *The Guardian*, 11 May 1999.

5. A similar argument is made by Doreen Massey in the editorial of *Soundings*, 7, Autumn 1997.

6. André Gorz, *Misères du présent, Richesse du possible*, Galilée, Paris, 1997.

7. Nikolas Rose, 'Community, Citizenship and the Third Way', in D. Meredyth and J. Minson (eds), *Citizenship and Cultural Policy*, London, 1999.

8. Michael Walzer, *Spheres of Justice*, New York, 1983.

9. This programme has been elaborated by the group which has launched the 'European Call for a Plural Citizenship and Plural Economy'. A presentation of their main theses can be found in Guy Aznar, Alain Caillé and others, *Vers une économie plurielle*, Paris, 1997.

CONCLUSION

THE ETHICS OF DEMOCRACY

I

The critique of the consensus approach elaborated in this collection of essays should not be understood as an endorsement of the view widespread among some 'postmodern' thinkers that democratic politics should be envisaged as an 'endless conversation' in which one should constantly try to enter into dialogical relations with the 'Other'. To be sure, those who advocate such a view usually insist, as I do, on the need to acknowledge 'differences' and on the impossibility of complete reabsorption of alterity. However, I think that in the end, like the deliberative model, they are unable to come to terms with 'the political' in its antagonistic dimension. This is not to underestimate their important divergences. While the deliberative democrats, with their emphasis on impartiality and rational consensus, tend to formulate the ends of democratic politics in the vocabulary of Kantian moral reasoning, the second view eschews the language of universal morality and envisages democracy not as a deontological but as an 'ethical' enterprise, as the unending pursuit of the recognition of the Other. To put it a bit schematically, we could speak of the opposition between moral-universalistic and ethical-particularistic approaches. The vocabulary of those who defend the 'ethical' perspective comes from a diversity of philosophical sources: Levinas, Arendt, Heidegger or even Nietzsche, and there are significant differences among them: but what is missing in all of them – as in the deliberative approach – is a proper reflection on the moment of 'decision' which character-izes the field of politics. This has serious consequences, since it is precisely those decisions – which are always taken in an undecidable terrain – which structure hegemonic relations. They entail an element of force and violence that can never be eliminated and cannot be adequately apprehended through the sole language of ethics or morality. We need a reflection of the political proper.

Let's be clear. I am not arguing that politics should be dissociated from ethical or moral concerns, but that their relation needs to be posed in a different way. I would like to suggest that this cannot be done without problematizing the nature of human sociability which informs most modern democratic political thinking. To grasp the shortcomings of the dominant view we need to go back to its origins: the period of the Enlightenment. A useful guide for such an enquiry is provided by Pierre Saint-Amand in *The Laws of Hostility*, a book where he proposes a political anthropology of the Enlightenment.[1] By scrutinizing the writings of Montesquieu, Voltaire, Rousseau, Diderot and Sade through the perspective developed by René Girard, he brings to the fore the key role played by the logic of *imitation* in their conception of sociability while, at the same time, unveiling its repressed dimension. He shows how, in their attempt to ground politics on Reason and Nature, the Philosophes of the Enlightenment were led to present an optimistic view of human sociability, seeing violence as an archaic phenomenon that does not really belong to human nature. According to them, antag-onistic and violent forms of behaviour, everything that is the manifestation of hostility, could be eradicated thanks to the progress of exchange and the development of sociability. Theirs is an idealized view of sociability that only acknowledges one side of what constitutes the dynamics of imitation. Pierre Saint-Amand indicates how in the *Encyclopedia* human reciprocity is envisaged as aiming exclusively at the realization of the good. This is possible because only one part of the mimetic affects, those linked to empathy, are taken into account. However, if one recognizes the ambivalent nature of the concept of imitation, its antagonistic dimension can be brought to light and we get a different picture of sociability. The importance of Girard is that he reveals the conflictual nature of mimesis, the double bind by which the same movement that brings human beings together in their common desire for the same objects is also at the origin of their antagonism. Rivalry and violence, far from being the exterior of exchange, are therefore its ever-present possibility. Reciprocity and hostility cannot be dissociated and we have to realize that the social order will always be threatened by violence.

By refusing to acknowledge the antagonistic dimension of imitation, the Philosophes failed to grasp the complex nature of human reciprocity. They denied the negative side of exchange, its dissociating impulse. This denial was the very condition for the fiction of a social contract from which violence and hostility would have been eliminated and where reciprocity could take the form of a transparent communication among participants. Although in their writings many of them could not completely elude the negative possibilities of imitation, they were unable to formulate conceptually its ambivalent character. It is the very nature of their humanistic project – the ambition to ground the autonomy of the social and to secure equality among human beings – that led them to defend an idealized view of human sociability.

However, says Saint-Amand, the fictitious character of this view was revealed by Sade, who denounced the idea of a social contract and celebrated violence. Sade can be seen as a form of 'aberrant liberalism' whose motto could be that private vices work towards the general vice. He cannot be separated from Rousseau, whose idea of a transparent community he reproduces in a perverted form: the general will becomes the voluptuous will and the immediacy of communication becomes the immediacy of debauchery.

II

The main lesson to be learned from this brief journey into the beginnings of our modern democratic perspective is that, contrary to what Habermas and his followers argue, the epistemological side of the Enlightenment is not to be seen as the precondition for its political side: the democratic project. Far from being the necessary basis for democracy, the rationalist view of human nature, with its denial of the negative aspect inherent in sociability, appears as its weakest point. By foreclosing the recognition that violence is ineradicable, it renders democratic theory unable to grasp the nature of 'the political' in its dimension of hostility and antagonism.

Contemporary liberals, far from offering a more adequate view of politics, are in a sense even less willing to acknowledge its 'dark side' than their forerunners. As we have seen, they believe that the development of modern society has definitively established the conditions for a 'deliberative democracy' in which decisions on matters of common concern will result from the free and unconstrained public deliberation of all. Politics in a well-ordered democratic society is, according to them, the field where a rational consensus will be established through the free exercise of public reason as in Rawls, or under the conditions of an undistorted communication as in Habermas. As I have shown in Chapter 4, they conceive political questions as being of a moral nature and therefore susceptible to a rational treatment. The aim of democracy is to establish procedures that would guarantee that an impartial point of view will be reached.

To begin thinking about democracy in a different way it is high time to understand that the critique of Enlightenment epistemology does not constitute a threat to the modern democratic project. We should take our bearings from Hans Blumenberg who, in *The Legitimacy of the Modern Age*, distinguishes two different aspects in the Enlightenment, one of 'self-assertion' and one of 'self-grounding'.[2] He argues that they have been joined historically but that there is no necessary relation between them and that they can be separated. It is therefore possible to discriminate between the idea of 'self-assertion' which is the truly modern side of the Enlightenment and the idea of 'self-grounding' which is merely a 'reoccupation' of a medieval position, that is, an attempt to give a modern answer to what is still a pre-modern question.

Following Blumenberg's lead allows us to grasp that rationalism, far from being essential to the idea of self-assertion, is in fact a residue from the absolutist medieval problematic. The illusions of providing itself with its own foundations which accompanied the labour of liberation from theology should now be abandoned and modern reason needs to acknowledge its limits. It is only by coming to terms with the radical implications of the pluralism of values (in its strong Nietzschean or Weberian version) and with the impossibility of a total harmony that modern reason frees itself from its pre-modern heritage.

III

An 'ethical' perspective is – potentially at least – more conducive to apprehending the limits of reason and to conceptualizing the plurality of values, and I certainly feel closer to the different approaches that speak in terms of 'ethics' instead of 'morality'. The problem with them, however, is that, while being generally more receptive to the role of rhetorics and persuasion and the importance of 'differences', they either avoid or do not emphasize enough the need to put some limits to pluralism, and they do not acknowledge the hegemonic nature of every possible consensus and the ineradicable violence that this implies.

I am not referring here to what I take to be a pre-modern form of 'ethical' discourse, the neo-Aristotelian ethics of the good advocated by the communitarians, whose inadequacy for a modern pluralist democracy I have already brought to the fore in *The Return of the Political*.[3] What I have in mind are the 'postmodern' ethical approaches which are critical of every attempt at reconciliation. In my view they fail to grasp the specificity of the political because they visualize the domain of politics through the lens of another language-game: the one of ethics. This is why their 'agonism' – contrary to the one I am advocating – has eliminated the antagonistic dimension which is proper to the political. The kind of pluralism they celebrate implies the possibility of a plurality without antagonism, of a friend without an enemy, an agonism without antagonism. As if once we had been able to take responsibility for the other and to engage with its difference, violence and exclusion could disappear. This is to imagine that there could be a point where ethics and politics could perfectly coincide, and this is precisely what I am denying because it means erasing the violence that is inherent in sociability, violence that no contract or dialogue can eliminate because it constitutes one of their dimensions. I submit that it is not through such a denial that democratic politics is to be secured and enhanced. On the contrary, it is by finally acknowledging the contradictory tendencies set to work by social exchange and the fragility of the democratic order that we will be able to grasp what I have argued is the task confronting democracy: how to transform the potential antagonism existing in human relations into an agonism.

IV

To elaborate my proposals for an 'agonistic pluralism' I have in the previous essays mobilized several theoretical discourses. Deconstruction I have found particularly helpful for criticizing what the consensus approach in all its variants – 'deliberative' as well as 'third way' – presupposes, the availability of a non-exclusive public sphere where a non-coercive consensus could be attained. Indeed, as Derrida shows, such an impartial stand-point is made structurally impossible by the undecidability which is at work in the construction of any form of objectivity. To see difference as the condition of the possibility of constitut-ing unity and totality, and at the same time as constituting their essential limits, forces us to acknowledge that alterity and otherness are irreducible. The deconstructive approach reveals that the vocabulary of Kantian universalist morality, in which the universality of moral imperatives is justified by their rational form, is profoundly inadequate for thinking about ethics and politics. Derrida has repeatedly insisted that, without taking a rigorous account of undecidability, it is impossible to think of the concepts of political decision and ethical responsibility.[4]

Undecidability, he says, is not a moment to be traversed or overcome, and conflicts of duty are interminable. We can never be completely satisfied that we have made a good choice since a decision in favour of some alternative is always at the detriment of another one. It is in that sense that deconstruction can be said to be 'hyperpoliticizing'. Politicization never ceases because undecidability continues to inhabit the decision. Every consensus appears as a stabilization of something essentially unstable and chaotic. Chaos and instability are irreducible, but this is at once a risk and a chance, since continual stability would mean the end of politics and ethics.

I would like, however, to express some reserves in order to differentiate my position from some appropriations of deconstruction which tend to read the idea of 'democracy to come' – which I have endorsed – as if it was a regulative idea, thereby eliminating its hard edge. How should we interpret it to avoid such a conflation? I suggest that it should be grasped in relation to what Derrida says when in *The Politics of Friendship* he scrutinizes the enigma of 'true friendship'.[5] As he indicates, two interpretations are possible: the first one conceives true friendship as an arche or a telos towards which one must strive, even if one never reaches it. The inaccessibility in this case is merely a distancing within the immensity of a homogeneous space; a road to be travelled. But such an inaccessibility can also be thought of in a second way, in terms of the alterity which makes true or perfect friendship not only inaccessible as a conceivable telos, but inaccessible because it is inconceivable in its very essence, and hence in its telos. Here inaccessibility takes the meaning of a prohibitive bar within the very concept of friendship. Quoting Pierre Aubenque, Derrida says that in this case one could say that 'perfect friendship destroys itself'. On the one hand we have therefore a conceivable, a determinable telos which in fact cannot be reached. On the other hand, the telos remains inaccessible because it is self-contradictory in its very essence.[6]

Envisaging the 'to come' of pluralist democracy along similar lines can help us to grasp the difference between the way democracy is conceived by a rationalist like Habermas and in the agonistic problematic which I am advocating. In the first case democratic consensus is conceived as an asymptotic approaching to the regulative idea of a free unconstrained communication, and the obstacles are perceived as being of an *empirical* nature. In the second case one acknowledges the *conceptual* impossibility of a democracy in which justice and harmony would be instantiated. Perfect democracy would indeed destroy itself. This is why it should be conceived as a good that exists as good only as long as it cannot be reached.

V

Is such an emphasis on the *conceptual* impossibility of reconciliation enough to come to terms with the ineradicability of antagonism? Does it provide the kind of ethical perspective that an agonistic conception of democracy requires? Several authors have recently argued that it is the 'ethics of psychoanalysis' as elaborated by Jacques Lacan which provides the kind of 'ethics of dis-harmony' called for by democratic politics. Slavoj Žižek has shown the role of Lacanian theory in undermining the very bases of an intersubjective communication free of constraints and violence.[7] Indeed Lacan reveals how discourse itself in its fundamental structure is authoritarian since, out of the free-floating dispersion of signifiers, it is only through the intervention of a master signifier that a consistent field of meaning can emerge. For him, the status of the master signifier, the signifier of symbolic authority founded only on itself (in its own act of enunciation), is strictly transcendental: the gesture that 'distorts' a symbolic field, that 'curves' its space by introducing a non-founded violence, is stricto-sensu correlative of its very establishment. This means that if we were to subtract from a discursive field its distortion, the field would disintegrate, 'de-quilt'.

Yannis Stavrakakis, for his part, indicates how, for Lacan, a crucial move by Freud is to deny the 'good as such' which has been the eternal object of the philosopher's quest in the field of ethics. He reveals that: 'What lies beyond the successive conceptions of the good, beyond the ways of traditional ethical thinking, is their ultimate failure, their inability to master the central impossibility, the constitutive lack around which human experience is organized.'[8] This impossibility is what he calls 'the Real' and the ethical strategy of psychoanalysis consists in the symbolic recognition of the irreducibility of the Real. Breaking with traditional ethics, the 'ethics of psychoanalysis' consists in dislocating the very idea of the good instead of proposing to reach harmony thanks to yet another conception of the good.

In a similar way, John Rajchman underlines what he calls the 'third revolution' introduced by Freud in the terrain of ethics and his breaking both with the perspective of ancient ethics, where the rules of duty revolved around the ends of virtue, and with the Kantian approach, which made the good revolve around the supreme principle of obligation. Freud derived a new sort of ethical concern and asked:

how we might be brought together not by prudence, abstract duty or calculated interest alone, but in our sharing the 'structure' of repression or the law which each makes his or her own according to the contingencies of his or her fortune – the structure of the 'decentered' subject and its response to the real. What sort of community can we have as divided subjects?[9]

As formulated by Lacan, the psychoanalytical approach opens a new series of questions for both ethical and political reflection, questions which converge with those which are at the core of the agonistic pluralism that I am advocating. It forces us, for instance, to face an important issue concerning the translation of the effects of the Real into socio-political analysis. If the Real is conceived not as an *effect* of a deeper ground but as operating in the very terrain of constitution of the social, its forms of appearance – antagonism, dislocation – cannot be reduced to a positive ground explaining them. This is what is involved in the idea – central to my argument – that social division is constitutive. More generally, this constitutive character of the Real involves a necessary displacement in the categories of classical ontology. New objects and relations between objects become thinkable, and this has crucial consequences for a non-rationalist understanding of the political.

As an ethics which strives to create among us a new form of bond, a bond that recognizes us as divided subjects, the psychoanalytical 'ethics of the Real' (Žižek) is, in my view, particularly suited to a pluralist democracy. It does not dream of an impossible reconciliation because it acknowledges not only that the multiplicity of ideas of the good is irreducible but also that antagonism and violence are ineradicable. What to do with this violence, how to deal with this antagonism, those are the ethical questions with which a pluralistic-democratic politics will for ever be confronted and for which there can never be a final solution.

Refusing to reduce the necessary hiatus between ethics and politics and acknowledging the irreducible tension between equality and liberty, between the ethics of human rights and the political logic which entails the establishment of frontiers with the violence that they imply, this is to recognize that the field of the political is not reducible to a rational moral calculus and always requires decisions. To discard the illusion of a possible reconciliation of ethics and politics and to come to terms with the never-ending interrogation of the political by the ethical, this is indeed the only way of acknowledging the democratic paradox.

NOTES

1. Pierre Saint-Amand, *The Laws of Hostility: Politics, Violence and the Enlightenment*, Minneapolis, 1996.

2. Hans Blumenberg, *The Legitimacy of the Modern Age*, Cambridge, MA, 1985.

3. Chantal Mouffe, *The Return of the Political*, London, 1993, Chapter 2.

4. See for instance his 'Remarks on Deconstruction and Pragmatism', in Chantal Mouffe (ed.), *Deconstruction and Pragmatism*, London, 1996, pp. 84–7.

5. Jacques Derrida, *The Politics of Friendship*, London, 1997, pp. 221–4.

6. This contradiction arises from the fact that one must want the greatest good for one's friend, that is, that she or he becomes a god. But one cannot want this for at least three reasons: (1) there is no longer the possibility of friendship with a god; (2) friendship commands us to love the other the way she or he is by wishing her or him to remain as she or he is. So one cannot deify a friend; (3) perfect or true friendship, that of the just and virtuous person who wishes to be like a god, tends towards divine autarkia which can easily do without the other and has no relationship to friendship.

7. See for instance Slavoj Žižek, *Enjoy Your Symptom!*, London 1992, Chapter 3.2, Identity and Authority.

8. Yannis Stavrakakis, *Lacan and the Political*, London, 1999, p. 129.

9. John Rajchman, *Truth and Eros*, New York, 1991, p. 70.

INDEX

Printed in the United States
By Bookmasters